EVERYDAY LIFE IN
ANCIENT EGYPT

W9-AGT-390

LIONEL CASSON

Everyday Life in Ancient Egypt

Revised and Expanded Edition

THE JOHNS HOPKINS UNIVERSITY PRESS
BALTIMORE AND LONDON

Originally published in 1975 as *The Horizon Book of Daily Life in Ancient Egypt.*

© 1975 by American Heritage, a division of Forbes Inc.

New material © 2001 The Johns Hopkins University Press

All rights reserved. Published 2001

Printed in the United States of America on acid-free paper

9 8 7 6 5 4 3 2 1

The Johns Hopkins University Press

2715 North Charles Street

Baltimore, Maryland 21218-4363

www.press.jhu.edu

Library of Congress Cataloging-in-Publication Data

Casson, Lionel, 1914–

Everyday life in ancient Egypt / Lionel Casson.—Rev. and expanded ed.

   p.   cm.

   Rev. ed. of: The Horizon book of daily life in ancient Egypt. 1975.

   Includes bibliographical references and index.

   ISBN 0-8018-6600-6 (alk. paper)

   ISBN 0-8018-6601-4 (pbk. : alk. paper)

   1. Egypt—Civilization—To 332 B.C. 2. Egypt—Social life and

customs—To 332 B.C. I. Casson, Lionel, 1914– Horizon book of

daily life in ancient Egypt. II. Title.

DT61 .C34 2001

932—dc21   00-059091

A catalog record for this book is available from the British Library.

To Alessia

CONTENTS

ILLUSTRATIONS

PREFACE

This book presents concise sketches of key aspects of
Egypt's people and their ways during the New Kingdom, roughly 1550
to 1075 B.C. This was a time of extended peace and great prosperity
whose remains, in particular the many tombs of pharaohs and nobles
tunneled into the living rock and lavishly decorated with wall paintings,
illumine vividly the daily life of the low as well as the high. The sketches
treat: the structure of Egyptian society; the nature of family life; the
place of women in the family and society; farming and what enabled it
to be the basic source of the country's wealth; religion, the role of the
afterlife, which demanded so much of an Egyptian's time and resources,
and the extraordinary effort of one heretical pharaoh to introduce radical religious change; the professions, whose members included engineers capable of raising such structures as the pyramids and the mighty
temples at Luxor and Karnak, and doctors so famed that they were in
demand abroad; and the crafts, whose practitioners turned out works
that today are treasured objects in museums all over the world.

The book originally appeared in 1975 as *Daily Life in Ancient Egypt.*
For this republication I have made a number of changes and adjust-
ments, mostly minor, added a chapter that reviews Egypt's history after
New Kingdom times, and supplied complete documentation (in a section at the end, keyed to the text by page numbers and brief clues).

EVERYDAY LIFE IN
ANCIENT EGYPT

CHAPTER I

The New Kingdom

They had a king who to them was a living god on earth, not merely heaven's chosen. They worshiped deities endowed with human bodies and animal heads or incarnated in crocodiles, bulls, cats, and other creatures, and they continued to do so long after they had become a sophisticated people. They were so hidebound that they maintained the same political forms, the same social structure, even the same style of art, for well-nigh three thousand years. No question about it, the Egyptians were a race apart.

One reason for this was the very special geography of their land. The Valley of the Nile was in truth a cradle of civilization, a place which assured the society that arose there an infancy snug and secure, unaffected by what went on in the regions round about. On three sides deserts formed a barrier, and on the fourth, the sea. Invaders who entertained the idea of breaking in by sailing down the Nile found six cataracts barring the way. The river, when properly handled, guaranteed the richest crops in the ancient world. In Upper Egypt the sun shone all day all year, while Lower Egypt received hardly more than a touch of rain; the Egyptians were blessedly ignorant of the violent weather that caused their contemporaries in Mesopotamia to make the god of storm their chief deity, or the Greeks across the water to refer to theirs as the Cloud-Gatherer and the Thunderer. They conceived of the world as stable and benign, and it is easy to see why, in their isolation and security, they did so.

One thing was required of them, cooperation. Since there was no rain, all water had to come from the river. Every year it flooded on schedule and provided plenty—so long as people worked together to build the dikes, canals, catch basins, and other devices needed to conserve it and were reasonable about sharing it. The Egyptians obviously worked well together, for we find them at a precocious age in their development forming ever expanding social and political entities, and eventually creating the first nation in history. It came into being when, about 3000 B.C., a semilegendary pharaoh named Menes took the final step of uniting Upper and Lower Egypt and thereby making the whole country into a single state; its capital he established at Memphis, not far from modern Cairo. From this moment on, Egyptian history marches along, dynasty after dynasty (it is traditional to divide its history into dynasties, periods when members of the same family ruled in succession), from the shadowy First Dynasty founded by Menes to the Thirtieth, the feeble kings of the mid–fourth century B.C. who held the throne during Egypt's last days as an independent state.

Once the land had been unified, it took but a few centuries to bring Egypt's culture into full flower. The Third to the Sixth dynasties, roughly 2675 to 2170 B.C., the period historians call the Old Kingdom, was an age in which her civilization was successful in a way that it would never be again, attaining heights it was never to reach again. This was when the Egyptians enjoyed to the full a style of life that was uniquely their own, totally free of influences from outside. This was when they were able to hold serenely to their conviction that the gods had set the world along a fixed and stable course, that the pharaoh in the nature of things ruled the land so that it was in harmony with this course, and that he could not do wrong; if things went awry—and even in the sunlit tranquillity of Old Kingdom Egypt they occasionally did—these were quite temporary interruptions that would inevitably soon be righted.

This was when everyone's place and purpose in life were clearly and simply defined: the pharaoh, a literal god on earth, owned all the land and disposed of the total energies of all his people. The high point of the Old Kingdom, and, in some ways, of Egypt's three-thousand-year career as a nation, was the Fourth Dynasty (about 2625–2500 B.C.), when pharaohs were able to call forth the labor, resources, and skills that produced the great pyramids to serve as their tombs.

Three centuries later the impossible had happened. The order that was supposed to be built into the nature of things had somehow become disorder—the god on earth no longer even ruled his land; he had been deposed, and Egypt was reduced to a cluster of little states, each under its own princeling. "This land is helter-skelter," wrote a so-called prophet in utter bewilderment, "and no one knows the result . . . I show thee the land topsy-turvy. That which never happened has happened." "Why, really, the land spins around as a potter's wheel does," wrote another. Law and order broke down so completely that people dared to ransack and burgle the holy of holies, the graves of their erstwhile god-kings. One writer expresses the disillusionment that swept the land with a bitter cynicism and alienation that could as easily come from a pen of the twentieth century A.D. as the twenty-second B.C.:

To whom can I speak today?
    Hearts are rapacious:
    every man seizes his fellow's goods.
(To whom can I speak today?)
    The gentle man has perished,
    (But) the violent man has access to everybody.
To whom can I speak today?
    (Even) the calm of face is wicked;
    goodness is rejected everywhere.
To whom can I speak today?
    (Though) a man should arouse wrath by
        his evil character,
    He (only) stirs everyone to laughter, (so)
        wicked is his sin. . . .

To whom can I speak today?
Faces have disappeared:
every man has a downcast face toward his
fellows.

Almost a century and a half passed before there was a return to the settled conditions that the Egyptians had once conceived to be eternally fixed. Some decades after 2100 B.C. the princelings of the little town of Thebes in Upper Egypt gathered the strength to conquer their competitors and reunite the kingdom. They transferred the capital to Thebes, which swiftly became a major city, and their dynasty, the Eleventh, launched the prosperous and successful period in Egyptian history known as the Middle Kingdom (1980–1630 B.C.). Powerful and able as the new rulers were, they could not turn back the clock. Egypt had been wounded mortally and was never to return to the serenity and confidence of Old Kingdom days. The difference is visible in the rendering of the pharaoh's image: the Old Kingdom rulers in their portraits gaze upon the world majestic and unruffled; those of the Middle Kingdom have careworn faces.

The Middle Kingdom was brought to a close by a weakening of the pharaoh's power accompanied by a misfortune that the Egyptians had never suffered before—invasion. About 1700 B.C. foreigners from Asia, the Hyksos, started infiltrating across the eastern desert and eventually took over much of Lower Egypt. Their disciplined units, using the most modern weapons of the day, overwhelmed the Egyptian soldiers, who were primitively armed and badly organized. A century and a half went by before there arose leaders, the founders of the Eighteenth Dynasty, who were able to drive out the enemy by teaching their people the use of his weapons and tactics. Once again Egypt became one land, this time to enter the most celebrated period of her history, the New Kingdom.

It lasted from roughly 1540 to 1075 B.C., the centuries when the Eighteenth, Nineteenth, and Twentieth dynasties held the throne, and it was marked by Egypt's conversion into a mighty international power.

Ancient Egypt.

There was no question now of remaining aloof from the world about her; in fact, her rulers aggressively made her a part of it. Hatshepsut, the first great queen of history, sent trade missions as far south as the coast of Ethiopia. Thutmose III, Egypt's Napoleon, founded a far-flung empire by leading his soldiers northward through Palestine, Lebanon, and Syria and sending his lieutenants into the Sudan to push the southern frontier down to the Fourth Cataract. With the proceeds of empire, Amenhotep III reared gorgeous palaces and lived in opulent splendor, while Ramses II during his long reign spangled the land with overblown temples and Brobdingnagian statues of himself.

This world was a far cry from the insular days of the Old Kingdom. The pharaoh maintained diplomatic relations with rulers in Crete, Cyprus, Asia Minor, the Levant, and his agents traded with all these places; there were Libyan, Sudanese, Asia Minor units in the army; nobles were served by slaves brought from foreign lands. Egypt became richer, more powerful, more flexible and varied, than she had ever been. In the process, however, she had to sacrifice much of what had made her so distinctive. The nation that had once prized isolation now was committed to daily intercourse with foreigners; the people whose basic tenets had been security and stability now lived amid the hazards of foreign involvements and threats and suffered from internal dissensions. Their king now acted like, and was treated as, an all-powerful autocrat rather than a god on earth.

Yet, in the face of it all, Egypt stubbornly remained Egyptian. The pharaohs raised the grandiose palaces and temples we flock to visit today, maintained the court whose nobles were laid to rest in the tombs that stud the hills about Thebes, set their myriad craftsmen to turning out the statues, reliefs, paintings, jewelry, furniture, and other objects that fill our museums. The temples are in the special Egyptian style; the sculptures, though they reveal the impact of new ideas, reverently follow age-old formulas; the gods that are portrayed are still the queer, primitive figures with animal heads upon human bodies. In the days of the New Kingdom Egypt was at her most variegated, mingling old with new, open on all sides to foreign influences but digesting them to produce results that are unmistakably native, keeping, despite all the changes, to fundamentally Egyptian ways.

It is this age that will chiefly concern us in the pages that follow. And an account of the Egyptians' daily life in these times can be given in far greater detail than for any other ancient nation, thanks to their distinctive attitude toward death and the rainless climate of the Nile Valley. The one led them to fashion their tombs in the likeness of their homes, to decorate them with scenes from the life the deceased had just left and would presumably continue to lead in the world beyond, and to fill them with all the objects they thought would be needed there. The other allowed all such objects, even delicate fabrics and frail sheets of papyrus paper, to lie unscathed under a blanket of dry sands for thousands of years. Egypt is a veritable storehouse of antiquity: no other place has preserved so rich a record of what its ancient inhabitants ate, wore, grew, worshiped, traded in, rode in, worked with, wrote with, fought with, amused themselves with, and so on. Theirs was a life of refinement and grace—at least for the upper classes. Looking at their pictures and writings, we need to remind ourselves that they lived in a civilization that seemed as ancient to the Greeks and Romans as that of the Greeks and Romans seems to us.

CHAPTER II

The Social Pyramid

Egypt's social structure formed a pyramid almost as neat as those built for her kings. It stood foursquare on the broad base of the mass of peasants who cultivated the rich land. Above them rose a series of narrowing layers: the mayors of the villages and their staffs, the governors of the various districts into which the country was divided for administrative purposes and their staffs, the ministers of state and other lofty officials at the capital, and, capstone of the whole, the pharaoh.

In theory the pharaoh owned all the land and controlled the total labor of the humble folk who worked it, and this very likely had been the practice in the awesomely autocratic days of the Old Kingdom. But in the sophisticated New Kingdom times, this simple arrangement remained only theory. The crown owned vast tracts of land, but so did religious foundations, notably that of Amon, the god who in this age ranked highest, and so did many of the pharaoh's officials, who made up the nobility of the kingdom. There were even relatively small-scale landowners. All had peasants tied to their land by habit and circumstance, if not by law, who worked on a sharecropping basis.

A New Kingdom pharaoh, constantly on view in the council chamber or at ceremonials or at the head of his troops, could no longer pretend to the divine majesty of his Old Kingdom predecessors. He was still, however, the highest religious figure in the realm, the link between his people and heaven, and so we find him tirelessly building new sanctuaries or restoring old ones, dutifully appearing at completion of the work for the inevitable formal dedications, granting gifts to this god, sacrificing to that.

For such occasions the imperial toilette must have taken hours. A noble as a matter of course was bathed, barbered, and pedicured daily; the pharaoh unquestionably had all this plus the donning of appropriate garb. His hair was kept short and he was clean-shaven, for wigs and a false beard were standard elements of the royal dress. Over the wigs he wore a selection of crowns, often the double crown, which combined those of Upper and Lower Egypt. His kilt was pleated and held up by a belt whose buckle bore his cartouche, the oval in which his name was written, done in elegant hieroglyphics. The royal jewelry included multiple ropes of pearls, bracelets, anklets—it must have been a physical burden to carry it all. Such regalia was *de rigueur* for court as well as religious ceremonials. There was, for example, the formal awarding of honors to deserving members of the administration and the army, when the pharaoh tossed the recipients gold necklaces, which they caught on the fly; or the formal reception of embassies from foreign lands, when the envoys made obeisance to His Majesty and presented a plethora of gifts, which were promptly inventoried by the court scribes and carted to the appropriate storage place.

Like many heads of state, the pharaoh gave over so much of his time to pure ceremony that he had to put the daily business of government in other hands. The office of vizier was created at least as early as the beginning of the Fourth Dynasty, about 2625 B.C. If the pharaoh was the captain of the Egyptian ship of state, the vizier was its executive officer, the man responsible for the working of the major branches of the administration. He was in charge of the treasury, supervising not only the taxes from Egypt but the tribute from her possessions or vassals abroad. He was in charge of public works, a position that under such frenetic builders as Amenhotep III or Ramses II must have claimed much of his attention. The pharaoh rode in glory at the head of the troops; it was the vizier who made sure that the royal guard was fully recruited and up to the mark, that the navy's units were ready for action. The pharaoh's word was law, but the actual administration of justice fell to the vizier. On top of all this, he had the duty of supervising the government's archives—and in a highly centralized state such as Egypt, with a bulging and busy bureaucracy, there was a formidable amount of paperwork. In Old Kingdom times one vizier sufficed, but the job grew so that during the New Kingdom there had to be two, a vizier for Lower Egypt stationed at Heliopolis (where Cairo's international airport now stands), and a vizier for Upper Egypt who stayed at the pharaoh's side in Thebes. The latter was the only official who had the right to be alone with the pharaoh; every day he met with him, to render a report and receive his orders.

The vizier had below him a network of lesser officials. The land was divided into some forty districts ("nomes"), and in Old and Middle Kingdom times these were administered by governors; in New Kingdom times the governors were replaced in importance by the mayors of the principal towns. After Egypt acquired possessions outside its borders, the territories in Asia were left in the hands of local rulers supervised by Egyptian commissioners, while the occupied part of Nubia was put under a viceroy with his own army and staff. All officials were responsible to the pharaoh by way of the vizier.

Next to the vizier in power were the top clerical figures, the high priests of Re, of Ptah, above all of Amon, who was the preferred god of the New Kingdom monarchs and received the lion's share of gifts and grants. Since these often took the form of land, the high priests came to control substantial revenues. Some estimates put the acreage that temple foundations held toward the close of the New Kingdom at 15 to 30 per cent of Egypt's agricultural land.

Inevitably, the pharaoh had about him a host of officials of lesser grade to take care of the myriad court and local duties. There was the Royal Chancellor, later the Chief Steward, who handled the palace revenues and administration down to arranging the tutoring of the royal children; the Overseer, or First Herald, often a retired soldier, in charge of palace ceremonial; a general manager of the living quarters and the table; the Overseer of the Harem, who supervised not only the great royal harems at Thebes, Memphis, and the Faiyum, but the traveling harem that accompanied the pharaoh on his journeys; and a multitude of lesser lights. The Egyptians were not averse to letting one person hold a number of posts, and men of ambition would collect them. Queen Hatshepsut's favorite courtier was a veritable Pooh-Bah: he managed to garner the posts of Overseer of the Fields, the Garden, the Cows, the Serfs, the Peasant-Farmers, and the Granaries of Amon; Prophet of Amon; Prophet of Amon's Sacred Barque; Chief Prophet of Montu in Hermonthis; Spokesman of the Shrine of Geb; Head Man in the House of the White Crown; Controller of the Broad Hall in the House of the Official; Steward of the King; Overseer of the Royal Residence; Great Father-Tutor of the Princess Nefru-Re; Controller of All Construction Work of the King in Karnak, plus a few others. Because it was the Egyptian way to keep good things within the family, there was a tendency for offices to be hereditary.

The royal family, together with the officials and clergy at the court, formed the upper crust of Egyptian society. Their circle was duplicated, on an appropriately smaller scale and lower level, by the local governor and his court in the various administrative districts and by the clergy at the religious foundations located elsewhere than in Thebes, such as Ptah's at Memphis or Re's at Heliopolis. The scribes made up another, rather self-important social stratum. The term is misleading since it includes white-collar workers of all levels and types, department managers, bureau heads, bookkeepers, collectors, and others, as well as clerks. The scribes of the imperial bureaucracy were the greatest in number and importance, but they were by no means the only ones. The army had its staff of them, so did the religious foundations, and any noble who owned extensive domains would have a number to take care of the necessary paperwork. The position of scribe, as we shall see, was one of the few avenues for upward movement in Egyptian society. The military provided another, but there the native Egyptian had to compete with foreigners, who came to form a large part of the armed forces.

Well below the scribes in social status were the artisans, a blanket term that covers the gamut of skilled workers, from the draftsmen who drew the plans for a temple or tomb through the artists who carved reliefs or painted pictures for its walls to the craftsmen who fashioned furniture, jewelry, and so on. To our way of thinking, the men responsible for Egypt's art deserve a far higher place in the social scale than the clerks who copied out, say, its tax records, but not to the Egyptian's. Artists were simply anonymous workmen who stood just above the peasant, the bottom level in their society.

In ancient Egypt's way of life, the various social strata did not live apart in distinctive areas but were intermingled within households or institutional complexes. Within the bounds of the palace there dwelt together the pharaoh, his queen, children, and the rest of the royal family; the officials of state whose duties required their close presence; many of the scribes employed in the central administration; the royal physicians; the royal guards; the valets, maids, and all others involved in the housekeeping; the bakers, brewers, butchers, cooks, scullions, and all others concerned with feeding the multitude that ate at the palace tables; the weavers and tailors who made the royal wardrobe; the sculptors who carved the royal portraits; the cabinet-makers who fashioned the royal furniture; drivers of the royal chariots, grooms of the royal stables, crews of the royal yachts, and so on. The new complex that Amenhotep III built on Thebes' west bank to accommodate them all sprawled over no less than eighty acres. The palace, in short, was a world in itself. And such worlds were repeated, on a smaller scale, in the households of the nobility, and on not so much smaller a scale, in the temple complexes. The staffs in these little worlds, from the top-ranking scribes to the lowliest drudge, were paid in kind (coinage was not to be invented until the seventh century B.C.), in the necessities of life, that is, specified quantities of grain, meat, oil, beer, unguents, flax, and the like. The quantities specified for a top-ranking scribe would enable him and his family to eat abundantly and dress handsomely; for a drudge, to fill his belly and cover his body. The supplies came from the estates that the household owned: the royal lands and herds furnished the palace's grain, flax, meat, hides; Amon's lands and herds did the same for the people in his temple complexes, and so on.

This distinctive social arrangement meant that Egypt had no urban communities in our sense, no conglomerations of people who lived together in mutual dependence, where shops and markets for exchanging goods and services were a permanent and prominent feature. Her cities and towns were clusters of the little worlds just described. The capital at Thebes was the mightiest of such clusters, boasting, in addition to the palace of the pharaoh and the households of various members of the nobility, the great temple institutions for Amon at Luxor and Karnak on the east bank of the river, and on the west bank those for the cult of the dead pharaohs. Also on the west bank was the housing project for the gangs of workers employed in hacking the royal tombs out of the sides of the Valley of the Kings and appropriately decorating them. Archaeologists have unearthed the crumbling remains of the seventy small mud-brick dwellings, laid out like a camp, that made it up.

As one descended the river from the First Cataract at Aswan, Egypt's traditional southern boundary, to the right and left along the ribbon of arable land that bordered the water was an unending line of these clusters, each marked by the gates and walls of the temple or palace that was its reason for being. At two points the farm area expanded: some thirty miles south of Memphis was the bulge of the Faiyum, originally a desert oasis embracing a large lake that the Egyptians early in their history linked up to the Nile by digging a canal; and just north of Memphis the river began fanning out to form its delta. In these two areas the clusters were dotted about, around the lake and along the tributaries.

How many people were there, all told, living in ancient Egypt? Some Greek and Roman writers report that, in its heyday, the country supported a population of seven to eight million, which gradually diminished to three million by the beginning of the Christian era. Three quarters of a century ago James Henry Breasted suggested that during the prosperous New Kingdom there were as many as five to six million, but those who have dealt with the problem in recent years are dubious; aware that the savants accompanying Napoleon during his invasion put the population then at merely two and a half million, they prefer a figure no higher than four to four and a half million. Whatever estimate one accepts, the total was but a fraction of the country's current population.

CHAPTER III

The Family

"If thou art a man of standing, thou shouldst found thy household and love thy wife at home as is fitting. Fill her belly; clothe her back. Ointment is the prescription for her body. Make her heart glad as long as thou livest. She is a profitable field for her lord [that is, to implant with seed]. . . . Let her heart be soothed through what may accrue to thee; it means keeping her long in thy house." Such was the advice of an Egyptian sage who wrote during the latter part of the Old Kingdom, about 2400 B.C. His opening words sum up the goals of an Egyptian male at all times: to marry and set up his own household. Since the Egyptians were first and foremost a practical people, the sage wisely adds tried and true means for keeping a wife happy: good food, clothes, perfume, and money.

The marriage of brother and sister, which ancient as well as modern writers on Egypt thought so noteworthy, was limited to the royal family, a means of ensuring the maximum amount of divine blood in the veins of a pharaoh's offspring. What counted in most marriages was status and dowry. The wife furnished one third of a couple's joint property, the husband the remaining two thirds, and who gave what was carefully recorded, since after the death of either party, though the survivor had the use of the whole, he or she could dispose only of the portion contributed. The prime purpose of every marriage was to produce children, especially boys. "Take to thyself a wife while thou art [still] a youth, that she may produce a son for thee," wrote a sage of late New Kingdom times in a list of instructions drawn up for his own son. For only a male offspring was entitled to carry on the family name and provide the proper rites for a dead father. This did not mean, however, that Egyptian parents slighted their daughters. The pharaoh Akhenaten, who, as will appear later, was particularly interested in putting his private life on display, shows himself and his wife dandling and nuzzling their little girls. In the many reliefs and paintings that reveal the importance of children in family life, we see both sexes flocking around their parents during their leisure moments, following them to work in the fields and being useful around the shops, as well as playing by themselves. Archaeologists have unearthed not only the usual run of children's toys—pieces of painted pottery, dolls, balls—but complicated toys that "work," such as a wooden lion whose mouth opens and shuts when a string is pulled or a wooden prisoner and dog on a pivot, which when properly manipulated has the dog biting at the man. The Greeks, accustomed to controlling family size by exposure of infants, marveled at the Egyptian practice of raising all children born—although they shrewdly noted that in such a rich and benign land, where children usually went around naked and could be fed boiled papyrus shoots or roots, the cost to the parents was negligible.

Soon after a child was born, it received a name, had its horoscope cast, and probably had the birth recorded in a local registry. Until infants were three, they were carried around by the mother in a sling hung about her neck and were the objects of her devoted care. The sage mentioned above includes in his instructions an admonition to his son to be kind to his mother, for "her breast was in thy mouth for three years continuously. Though thy filth was disgusting, her heart was not disgusted, saying 'What can I do?' She put thee into school when thou wert taught to write, and she continued on thy behalf every day, with bread and beer in her house."

Children of upper-class families not only had the advantage of receiving an education, but grew up in very attractive homes, as we can tell from pictures on the walls of the tombs of the wealthy as well as from actual remains, particularly those that have been unearthed amid the ruins of the new city that Pharaoh Akhenaten built for himself at Tell el Amarna. They were spacious dwellings set amid ample grounds in estates surrounded by high, thick walls to ensure privacy. The home of a well-to-do family had an imposing front porch garnished with columns, yet another columned porch, and in the center of the house a large, formal living room with a roof supported by no fewer than four columns and in exceptional cases by more. This room, which rose higher than those around it, was lighted by clerestory windows, rectangular openings covered by a stone grill, just below the ceiling. From the living room a staircase led to the roof. Behind it lay the master bedroom, with an alcove for the bed and within easy reach a bathroom and lavatory. The bathroom was a small chamber, a corner of which was floored and lined with stone; here the bather was sluiced down by his servants, and nearby was a chair where he sat while being massaged. Next to the bathroom was the lavatory, which boasted a brick seat with a rectangular hole made by leaving out a few bricks, and under it a removable pot. One refinement was to have a wooden instead of a brick seat. Around and about were numerous smaller chambers, presumably for the rest of the family, and a square room, its roof supported by a single column, that was the family sitting room. A separate building set against the circuit wall housed the kitchen. Also along the wall were servants' quarters, stalls for a few cows, poultry shed, bins for storage. Walls were of sundried brick with mud plaster, whitewashed or decorated with murals; the thresholds and jambs of the outside doorways were of stone; roofs were of wooden beams with crosspieces at right angles to support a covering of mud plaster; columns were of painted wood on stone bases; floors were of whitewashed or painted brick. Much of the space between the house and the circuit of the walls was given over to the garden, formally laid out with square or rectangular plots divided by tree-lined paths, a pool in which papyrus and lotus grew and which might be big enough to accommodate a boat, and pergolas to offer shady seating areas.

Middle-class houses were smaller and simpler. In town they stood side by side, with a single columned porch and an interior court substituting for the garden that the Egyptian homeowner so treasured. The ground floor was usually given over to workrooms for spinning, weaving, grinding grain, baking bread, and brewing beer. On the first floor were the dining and living rooms, illuminated by small square windows, while the bedrooms were on the floor above. The roof was flat, surrounded by a parapet. It was much used for housing storage bins, for doing household chores, passing the cool of the evening, or sleeping alfresco.

Artisans and their families crammed into tiny houses. In one workers' village that has been excavated there were two to three hundred dwellings in an area little more than 250 by 100 yards. The housing that we know best is contained in the ruins at Tell el Amarna, site of the new city of Pharaoh Akhenaten. For the gangs assigned to hacking out tombs nearby, he built a model village, an example of Egyptian town planning. The houses, lining both sides of a straight street, were as monotonously alike as their modern equivalents. Each was about 16½ feet wide by about 33 feet long. From the street one entered a shallow room, running the breadth of the house, which was used for stabling animals or as a workroom or in some cases, as we shall see in a moment, for cooking. Behind was the living-dining room, also as wide as the house, with its roof supported by a column; a big jar containing the family water supply was kept there. The rear third was divided by a cross wall into two tiny chambers, one a bedroom and the other a kitchen. Unfortunately the architects, with a remissness that seems congenital in the profession, forgot to allow for the mandatory staircase to the roof. Some houseowners added it in the kitchen, which meant that they had to climb a few steps to get at the bread oven and bump against the fireplace to get upstairs. Others who did not happen to need their front room for animals or work space set up their kitchen there, abandoning the rear chamber to the staircase. Tight as these quarters were, they no doubt were better than what the peasants had; they must have lived as they still do in places today, in a hovel shared with their beasts.

Whether sumptuous or simple, houses were kept clean; the Egyptians were punctilious about this. To judge from the recipes that are included in their medical writings, they even did their best to rid their homes of pests. A solution of natron, the soda that is found in abundance in Egypt, was recommended for driving off insects, natron or onion seeds placed around a snake's hole for keeping the creature safely inside, oriole grease for use against flies, fish spawn against fleas. Cat grease smeared on sacks was supposed to drive off rats, and a solution of gazelle dung smeared on the walls and floor of a grain bin was good against all sorts of rodents.

The chief article of furniture was the chair, ranging from the gorgeous thrones of the pharaohs, through the high-backed handsomely carved armchairs favored by the well-to-do, down to simple stools, including a folding kind with a leather or woven seat. Often they were very low, a mere foot or so off the ground, designed for people who were used to squatting on the floor. Dining rooms did not have a single large table but a number of smaller ones, since Egyptians, even in company, preferred to eat singly or in pairs. The finest dinnerware was of gold and silver or delicately made and highly decorated pottery. Toward the end of our period bronze drinking and serving vessels were much favored. A bed consisted of a wooden frame that supported a mesh or network of cord over which the mattress was laid; the Egyptians with their native practicality had even developed a type of bed that folded in half very much the way some of ours do. Good bedrooms usually had wooden chests for linen and clothes. Workers' and peasants' homes made do with simple and minimal furnishings: there rush mats served as beds, stools and tables were of stone, and tableware was of roughhewn wood or coarse pottery.

Every household of any pretension had its staff of servants: valets for the master, maids for the mistress, miscellaneous help to do the grinding, baking, cooking, spinning, weaving, and other chores. Servants were both free and slave, the latter usually captives of war or their descendants. Civil status by no means reflected rank. Foreign slaves often occupied the highest posts in a home, serving as major-domos, personal valets, attendants in the harem, and the like. Though slaves, they were infinitely better off than the free peasant: they lived in far roomier and richer quarters, ate better, and if talented stood a good chance of moving upward in the household hierarchy. All the staff—free and slave, native and foreign—had to keep a sharp eye out for the master's or their superior's stick, since this was the Egyptian's sovereign device for getting things done, and he used it liberally and indiscriminately on all living creatures about him, from his domestic animals to his wife. It was a great distinction for a man of less than the highest birth to boast that he had never been beaten in the presence of his betters.

And there were pets. The Egyptians concurred with the well-nigh universal feeling that the dog was man's best friend. One pharaoh had his favorite four carved in stone, and we find graves of dogs mingled with those of dwarves, archers, and women in the burial grounds at Abydos. During the period we are concerned with, two breeds were in vogue, a small dachshundlike species for lap dogs and hounds for hunting. Cats were common, including the brindled tabby. So were monkeys, which are frequently pictured scurrying about the rooms and garden. So too were Nile geese, which is a surprise since, being greedy, noisy, and aggressive, they are hardly amiable creatures.

Egyptians, like most ancient peoples, generally lived by the sun, rising at dawn and going to sleep shortly after nightfall. There were sophisticated means for telling time, sundials in the daytime and instruments for observing the stars at night, and water clocks for measuring the passing of time, but all were almost exclusively for use by the priests in their religious functions.

The Egyptian began his day, as we do, by washing; he was as fussy about the cleanliness of his body as of his house. "They always wear freshly washed linen clothes; they make a special point of this. They have themselves circumcised for reasons of cleanliness, preferring cleanliness to a more attractive appearance. Priests shave their bodies all over every other day to keep off lice or anything else dirty. . . . They bathe in cold water twice a day and twice every night." So reported Herodotus, who visited the land sometime about the middle of the fifth century B.C., and even if he has exaggerated ideas of the habits of Egyptian priests, the emphasis on personal hygiene is clear enough. Soda was the cleanser used in lieu of soap, which was still unknown, and rich and poor alike rubbed the body with ointments to counteract the drying effect it had on the skin. When the work gangs at Thebes' necropolis went out on strike about 1170 B.C., one of their key grievances was that their ration of ointment had not been paid. The well-to-do, in addition to skin softeners, went in for perfumes and deodorants. They had an unguent of pine oil and incense compounded with powder and scented for rubbing all over, and there were special concoctions for applying under the armpits and in the crotch. At parties all the women and some of the men fastened on top of their heads a cone of pomade which, as it melted, perfumed the hair.

The master and mistress of a wealthy household, as mentioned earlier, followed their ablutions by a session with the barber or hairdresser, and then with the servant who made them up, for both sexes used cosmetics. There was green eye paint of powdered malachite (ore of copper) to touch up the brows and the corners of the eye and give it the almond shape that was *comme il faut,* black eye paint, resembling kohl, of powdered galena (ore of lead) to apply to the rims and lashes, red ocher mixed with tallow or vegetable grease for lipstick, red juice of the henna plant to tint the fingers and toenails. Ladies of fashion as well as men had razors (of bronze) to get rid of unwanted hair, and for both the hand mirror, a highly polished bronze disk with a handle, was an essential toilet article. There were all sorts of beauty aids: to remove pimples, to smooth out wrinkles, above all to cure baldness. The castor oil plant, for example, whose laxative properties were known and utilized, was equally in demand as a hair restorer. Rare fats were also thought to be effective "to cause hair to grow on a bald person"; for this purpose the fat of a lion, hippopotamus, crocodile, cat, snake, and ibex were mixed together. For the elderly who had managed to keep their hair, there were remedies against its turning gray, such as rubbing in a mixture of oil with the blood of a black calf or ox or the fat of a black snake. One exotic prescription called for the womb of a female cat, a raven's egg, oil, and laudanum boiled together. All, to quote a ranking authority on the history of medicine, "were probably as effective and ineffective as our present innumerable hair tonics."

There were all-purpose lotions as well, such as an oil derived by a complicated recipe that started with ground fenugreek: it cured baldness, removed freckles, crow's-feet, and other skin blemishes, and, on top of that, helped "change an old man into a young one." Only the well-to-do, to be sure, had the time and money to spend on such matters. A middle-class housewife did her own hair, while peasants made matters simple by shaving theirs off. We have a picture of them lined up awaiting their turn as an itinerant barber, who has set up his stool under a tree, shaves a customer, leaving him with a cranium as smooth and shiny as a billiard ball.

The Egyptians, with no inhibitions about displaying the body, dressed for the climate. Almost all garments were of linen woven from the flax that was one of the land's important agricultural products. The story of Sinuhe, a political refugee who spent long years in Syria before returning home, tells of the hero's relief when he was finally able to doff his heavy Syrian wool clothing for the cool comfort of Egyptian linen. At home a man wore but a kilt and walked around barefoot. When going out he added sandals of leather or plaited papyrus, a short-sleeved shirt, jewelry—strings of beads of faience or semiprecious stones such as jasper and lapis lazuli, seal rings, armlets, bracelets—and perhaps exchanged his kilt for a full-length skirt or put one on over the kilt; the skirt might be adorned with pleats. Over this he might wear an ankle-length short-sleeved robe of linen cloth, it too sometimes pleated, held in about the waist by a narrow sash. The usual dress for a woman was a sleeveless form-fitting sheath that reached to the ankles. For social occasions it was pleated and almost incredibly sheer; the neckline varied and could be cut so low as to reveal the breasts. Over it, like the men, she might wear a robe, sometimes gathering it around the left breast so as to reveal the right. Both men and women donned full wigs for banquets and ceremonies. At these the coolest of all were the young serving girls, for they waited on the guests in nothing more than a wig and some jewelry. Peasants, artisans, and laborers made do with just a kilt, though on festival days they would trick themselves out with trinkets of faience or even bronze. Children were sensibly allowed to go about naked.

At dinner parties the tables were piled so high one wonders how the lovely slender ladies who are shown seated at them kept their figures. As a matter of fact, statues of the middle-aged traditionally show rolls of belly fat; it was the mark of the successful man.

Egyptians did most of their cooking over open hearths on a fire of charcoal or wood or, in poor homes, of reeds, straw, or cow dung. Meat and poultry were boiled or stewed in earthenware pots or roasted on spits. In practically all households, even the modest ones of workers, flour was ground and bread baked at home, the women or servants daily going through the laborious chore of milling the grain by hand and sifting it. Every kitchen in addition to a hearth had its bake-oven, a cylindrical affair made of a large pot plastered over with mud. The dough was pressed into a mold and set inside. Breads of various shapes and quality were turned out, as well as pastries made by adding honey, milk, fat, or butter. On farm estates flour, often of barley, was ground for brewing as well as baking, since beer was the national drink. Only the upper classes enjoyed their glass of wine, which was more expensive because it came from the delta, the one place in Egypt where the climate favored the growing of grapes.

Egyptians ate more beef than other ancient peoples. Cattle were raised extensively, and some pictures show them so fattened that they seem scarcely able to walk. Then there was game from the desert, oryx, gazelle, antelope. In Old Kingdom times efforts had been made to domesticate these creatures, but by our period such attempts had been given up. Poultry was not only standard on farms, but any house in town with the room had its poultry shed. The breeds included ducks, geese, and pigeons, occasionally quail, but not chickens, which were either rare or unknown. Game birds were a common dish on the tables of the rich, water fowl from along the river or the marshes of the delta. The river yielded numerous varieties of fish, but these were eaten mostly by the poor, since there were taboos against fish—certain types were explicitly prohibited at certain times in certain villages and districts—that the well-to-do could afford to respect. Meats, poultry, and fish could be eaten right away or kept by curing and drying. Vegetables included peas, beans, lettuce, onions, leeks, garlic. Fruits were limited: dates, figs, grapes, pomegranates, and a few others. Honey and carob seeds were the sweeteners.

The poor enjoyed meat, poultry, and fruits only at festival times, when the god being honored graciously furnished public banquets. Their everyday fare was, then as now, bread, onions, and leeks, washed down with beer or just plain water. When times were hard they turned to eating boiled papyrus shoots or roots or chewing papyrus pith.

Egyptian families went to bed soon after dusk. For illumination during the short interval between nightfall and bedtime they had lamps in the form of a simple saucer of pottery or stone swimming with castor oil or linseed oil or sesame oil in which a braided linen wick floated. Candles were for the temples; the oil lamp was the ubiquitous form of lighting, used not only by households but by the workers engaged in hacking out underground tombs and by the intruders in robbing them.

So far as we can tell, it was the Egyptians who gave to the world that most useful of devices, mosquito netting. People living in the delta had to contend with the insect life that throve in the marshes and came out at night in swarms. When Herodotus visited the area he observed that "everyone owns a net, which during the day he uses for catching fish but at night as follows. He sets the net up around the bed where he takes his rest, then creeps inside and sleeps under it. If he sleeps wrapped in a cloak or linen garment, insects bite through, but they don't even try to bite through a net."

CHAPTER IV

Women

To keep the royal line as pure as possible, pharaohs most often married women of royal blood. Thus the queen of Egypt usually was, at one and the same time, daughter of a god, wife of a god, and mother of a god—enough to give her exceptional status among a people who, as elsewhere in the ancient world, took male dominance for granted. So exceptional was it that, as in few other nations, it led to the acceptance of queens as rulers of the land—though only when there was no male heir. To satisfy appearances, they customarily represented themselves as "female kings."

As far back as Old Kingdom times there were women of the royal family of sufficient importance to be buried with pharaohlike splendor. Toward the end of the Old Kingdom, shortly after 2300 B.C., Pepi II ascended the throne as a mere boy of six, and for a number of years his mother ruled as regent. He died after a reign of nearly a century, so feeble in his last years that the erstwhile awesome pharaonic authority lost its magic, leading to the disorders that brought the Old Kingdom to an ignominious end. During its final days there were a number of short-lived pharaohs, one of whom, Nitocris, was the first queen to hold a throne in the annals of history. She lasted only two years, and if we can believe a story that was still going the rounds almost two millenniums later, when Herodotus picked it up from some priests he talked with, she was herself responsible for its brevity. Gaining the crown by the will of the people after the murder of her brother had removed the male incumbent, "she had," says Herodotus, "a large underground chamber built. Giving out that she was going to inaugurate it, but with other ideas in mind, she invited to a banquet there many whom she knew to be the chief ones responsible for her brother's murder. While they were feasting, she let in the river water on them through a big concealed pipe." "The only other thing I was told about her," he concludes, "was that, after carrying this out, she threw herself into a room full of ashes [where she presumably smothered] to escape her punishment." A later and rather more gallant historian remarks that she was "the noblest and loveliest woman of her time."

A good deal more is known about Egypt's greatest queen, Hatshepsut, who came to the throne about 1500 B.C. and held it for almost two decades. She was the daughter of a pharaoh, Thutmose I, the wife of a pharaoh, Thutmose II, but only the stepmother of the boy she supplanted, who was to succeed her as Thutmose III and become the founder of the Egyptian empire. She seems to have begun as regent for him and gradually promoted herself, ultimately ruling with full right as "king" of all Egypt. Her statues sometimes portray her as a man, decked out in male clothing and wearing the pharaoh's traditional false beard, and sometimes allude to her femininity by rendering her breasts. On the vast and beautiful tomb-temple she built for herself at Deir el-Bahari, across the river from Thebes, she inscribed an illustrated account of what she considered her chief accomplishments. Befitting a woman, they were not acts of war but of peace, notably a large-scale trading expedition to Punt (Ethiopia or Somalia), whence Egypt imported incense and certain other products. When her stepson finally got the

FACING PAGE: An upperclass woman elegantly dressed in white linen. She has an incense cone upon her head.

throne he paid off her presumption by knocking over her statues and hacking out her name from her inscriptions.

Though there were to be no more "female kings," women continued to play a key role at Egypt's court. Amenhotep III, a pharaoh with a penchant for grand gestures, deliberately bypassed the eligibles of the royal line to choose for his queen a certain Tiy, the daughter of an obscure family. He had her portrayed as of equal importance in the statue groups he commissioned, linked her name with his in public announcements, built her a temple where the cult of her image was carried on, and, merely as a gift for her, had a lake dug that measured more than a mile long and a fifth of a mile wide. After he died she frequently received communications from heads of the states with which Egypt had diplomatic relations. But even her prominence falls short of her daughter-in-law's. Nefertiti is the one Egyptian queen most of us know about, and this is solely due to the attention her husband, the unconventional pharaoh who broke away from so many Egyptian traditions, paid her, the portrait heads he had the court sculptors make of her, the prominence he gave her in the reliefs illustrating his activities.

But a queen's place in the scheme of things is, of course, a far cry from that of her less exalted sisters. The position of Egyptian women presents an anomaly. On the one hand, Egypt's society was typically male-dominated: the word of the man of the house was law, and a wife was in many ways her husband's chattel. On the other hand, Egyptian women enjoyed far more rights and privileges than in other lands, modern as well as ancient.

First, on the debit side, Egyptian wives had to share their husbands with other women. Every pharaoh had a harem; the queen was his "Great Wife," enjoying an acknowledged and official status higher than the members of his harem. We hear of several harem intrigues arising from the attempts of the ladies to promote the fortunes of their own sons, and there surely were many others that have escaped the notice of history. The coffins of five members of the harem of Mentuhotep II, a ruler of the Eleventh Dynasty, have been found; each of the five bore an inscription asserting that the inmate was the king's favorite.

Probably few Egyptian husbands except for the pharaoh could afford a harem, but most had several wives or concubines, although in all cases there was one official primary wife. Statues, reliefs, and paintings traditionally show her in an affectionate pose with her husband, her arm over his shoulder or about his waist; yet in the regular course of things she usually had no sole claim on his embraces. Those she shared them with had their own problems, for they were permanently locked into a subordinate position that could leave them helplessly open to humiliation. A letter is preserved, dating from about 2000 B.C., in which the writer, a wealthy man who was off visiting some of his properties in the north, orders his sons at Thebes to "have the housemaid Senen turned out of my house at once. . . . Behold, if Senen spends a single day in the house, thou wilt be to blame if thou lettest her do harm to my concubine. What am I supporting thee for and what can my concubine do to you, you fine boys? . . . And as to doing harm to my concubine, take warning!" Clearly the writer somehow got wind that, in his absence, the household, sons and servants, were ganging up on the poor girl.

At banquets wives and husbands were usually seated separately, women with women and men with men. A husband who was angry with his wife could banish her to her quarters; in a legal document that has come down to us a woman prefaces her testimony before a court with the remark, "May I be sent to the back of the house if I speak not the truth." And of course he could beat her—within limits; if it could be proved that he had gone too far, he had to swear never to do it again under penalty of receiving one hundred lashes and forfeiting his contribution to their joint property. Some men, when they went up in the world, unscrupulously shucked off the women of modest origins whom they had married before their prospects were so bright; at least this is the distinct impression left by the way a widower in a letter addressed to his dead wife insists that he "rose to the highest rank but I never deserted you. . . . I never deserted you from my youth to the time when I was holding all manner of important posts for Pharaoh. . . . When anyone came to talk to me of you, I would not heed the advice he gave me about you." The man's worldly and practical friends must have been telling him that he could do better.

As in so many societies, an Egyptian woman paid for adultery with her life, even by burning, whereas it was no crime at all for a male. Like so many literatures, the Egyptian portrays men as upstanding, heroic, and true, and women as frivolous, spiteful, and false. A wife on the loose was supposed to be always ready to cheat on her husband. "Be on thy guard against a woman from abroad, who is not known in town," the sage whom we have had occasion to quote earlier warns his son. "Do not stare at her when she passes by. Do not know her carnally: a deep water, whose windings one knows not, [is] a woman who is far away from her husband. 'I am sleek,' she says to thee every day. She has no witnesses when she waits to ensnare thee."

Now let us turn to the credit side. The statues and reliefs and pictures that portray the "togetherness" of man and wife, or that show the wife playing the important role of mistress of the household, are not mere concessions to a time-honored artistic formula. They mean what they show; Egyptian husbands were aware that it took two to make a marriage. "Thou shouldst not supervise thy wife in her house, when thou knowest she is efficient," the sage goes on to tell his son. "Do not say to her: 'Where is it? Fetch it for us!' when she has put it in the most useful place. Let thine eyes have regard, while thou art silent, that thou mayest recognize her abilities. How happy it is when thy hand is with her!" In ancient Greece women were second-class creatures who led lives apart, closed off in a special area of the house; entertaining, sports, even casual passing of the time, were for men only, as in Islamic countries today. In ancient Egypt husband and wife chatted together, played games together, threw parties together—she even went along on his hunting forays to keep him company. Egyptian women shared with men important legal rights that in many another nation were totally denied them: they were allowed to own land, operate businesses, not only testify in court but bring actions against men.

There is no question that marriages were arranged by parents and that the chief considerations were family and property and the prime purpose the raising of sons. Yet, among the rags and tatters of Egyptian literature that have survived, there are a number of love poems which make no sense unless we will grant that there was at least some element of romance in Egyptian marriages. Here, for example, is the lament of a boy who was literally lovesick with yearning for his "sister" (lovers referred to each other as "sister" and "brother"):

Seven days to yesterday I have not seen the sister,
    and a sickness has invaded me;
my body has become heavy,
    (and I am) forgetful of my own self.
If the chief physicians come to me,
    my heart is not content with their remedies. . . .
What will revive me is to say to me: "Here she is!"
    Her name is what will lift me up. . . .
My health is her coming in from outside:
    When I see her, then I am well. . . .
When I embrace her, she drives evil away from me—
    But she has gone forth from me for seven days!

In another poem a girl who has fallen in love with the boy next door desperately hopes that her mother will come to her aid: "Though he lives close by my mother's house, yet I cannot go to him," she laments. "It would be kind of my mother to undertake that for me. . . . If he would but send some message to my mother! My brother, I have vowed myself to thee, as thy bride to be. . . . Come to me that I may see thy beauty!" The girl actually takes matters in her own hands and has no trouble getting her man. "She came of her own accord to see me!" exclaims the boy. "How wonderful is my lot! I exult, I rejoice, I am exalted!" But the parents' consent is mandatory, and the girl is on tenterhooks until it is forthcoming:

I passed close by the open door of his house. My brother was standing beside his mother, with all his brothers and sisters. . . . He looked upon me as I passed, but I had none to share my joy. My heart rejoices in full measure that my brother has seen me. God grant that his mother may know my heart; then she would come to visit me. Oh, Noubit [goddess of joy and love], put this thought in her heart! I run to my brother and I kiss him nose to nose [Egyptians kissed by rubbing noses], before his companions.

If, as such poems seem clearly to indicate, love went into the making of a marriage as well as family and property, then Egyptian women of the second millennium B.C. did indeed enjoy a dimension of freedom greater than any of their sisters from other places in ancient times.

CHAPTER V

On the Farm

"Egypt . . . is . . . the gift of the Nile," noted Herodotus. The great river, from Khartoum on flowing through a valley gashed in desert, creates in the midst of sterility an elongated oasis that from prehistoric times gave not merely life but a good life to the Egypt of the pharaohs.

Each year the main stream, swollen with the torrential rains that fall in Ethiopia, rushes north to flood its valley. "When the Nile inundates the land," wrote Herodotus, "all of Egypt becomes a sea, and only the towns remain above water, looking rather like the islands of the Aegean. At such times shipping no longer follows the course of the river but goes straight across the country. Anyone, for example, traveling from Naucratis to Memphis sails right alongside the pyramids." As the waters recede, they leave behind a layer of fertile silt—"black land" the Egyptians called it to distinguish it from the barren "red land" of the desert. Egyptians never had to scan the skies anxiously for signs of rain; every summer the Nile provided irrigation. They never had to let fields lie fallow to keep from exhausting the soil; every summer the Nile refreshed it.

The river, to be sure, was not always a blessing. If the annual flood was too high, the spreading waters brought ruin; if too low, they missed marginal areas and less land was available for the plow. If they were too low for several years in a row, there was famine. Joseph's interpretation of the pharaoh's dream as portending seven fat years and seven lean was based not on fancy but on what happened along the Nile.

The Egyptians divided the year into three seasons rather than four, according to the behavior of their river. "Inundation," the time of the flood, lasted roughly from June through September; "Emergence of the fields from the waters," when the water drained off leaving the soil moist, lasted from October until about February; and "Drought" went on from then until June, when the cycle began all over again. During the Emergence the peasants caught and hoarded the fast-receding waters and planted in the mud. Drought was when they harvested and threshed. During the Inundation, when the flood prevented any work on the fields, they were free to work on the pharaoh's building projects.

It took a full-scale and thoroughly organized effort to harness the river. Up and down the land men threw up and maintained dikes to protect their villages against being inundated, laid out catch basins to trap water as the flood receded, dug canals from these so that when needed the water could be released upon the fields. They set up Nilometers—gauges to measure the rise—at Cairo and the First Cataract, and then, as Egypt's boundaries were extended into the Sudan, farther up the river—the pharaoh wanted the earliest possible notice of what the national fate for the year would be.

The Nile watered the land and refreshed it, enabling it to produce in such abundance that Herodotus and the authors of the Bible wrote in wonder of the fleshpots of Egypt. Its behavior determined real-estate values, for farm land was divided into that which always received the benefits of flooding, that which sometimes did, and that which never did; taxes were assessed accordingly. It determined many of the cases that came to court, for there were incessant wrangles over the use of water. It determined even what men did in the hereafter: when an Egyptian faced the tribunal of the afterworld, of equal importance to his avowal that he had not killed or robbed was his declaration that he had not "held up the water in its season" or "built a dam against running water."

The Egyptians used the fertile mud to grow first and foremost wheat and barley for their bread and beer. Reversing the normal procedure, they sowed and then plowed, merely to turn up the soft earth in order to cover the seed. No great force was required, so their plows were feeble affairs made of wood and drawn by a yoke of cows—not oxen, whose massive strength was saved for hauling blocks of stone. Sometimes the peasant even dispensed with plowing and simply turned a herd of light animals, sheep or pigs, loose in the field to trample in the seed. In either case it had to be done in a hurry, before the ground lost its moisture and began to harden. As the crops ripened under the hot sun, the peasants irrigated them by opening the canals from the catch basins and letting the water run through onto the planted areas.

Harvest time brought into the fields not only the peasants en masse but the master himself or his agent and a swarm of his scribes, for nothing important was done in Egypt without paperwork, and the checking and measuring of the grain crop was just about the most important matter there was. While the scribes set out their inkpots, pens, and scrolls in shaded comfort under a tree, the line of reapers got to work, wielding wooden sickles with flint teeth. They cut the grain high, leaving a long stubble, and women with baskets followed behind to gather up what had been cut. In their wake came the gleaners, women, children, old men. One tomb painting shows a woman gleaner pathetically holding out her hand and saying, "Give me just a handful. I came last evening. Don't make my luck as bad today as it was yesterday." Another picture, in a lighter vein, shows two girls pulling each other's hair in a fight over the gleanings while the reapers unconcernedly carry on their work. The sheaves were carried off to the threshing floor by donkeys or men. The floor, of beaten earth, was covered over with a thick layer of stalks and ears, and oxen were made to tread on it. Gangs then separated the straw with forks and winnowed the chaff with scoops. The last step was to store the grain in the silos, and this was done under the gimlet-eyed supervision of inspectors, with scribes jotting down the figures as the precious stuff was measured out to make sure that no peasant cheated his master or the state out of a kernel. Anyone who did was summarily laid out on the ground and thrashed.

Other major crops were flax for linen, and castor beans and sesame for oil, but none came near grain in importance. Raising vegetables and fruits was all small scale, done in the house gardens.

One crop that was extensively harvested was supplied by nature with no effort on the farmers' part—papyrus reeds, the celebrated bulrushes from which the ark for the infant Moses was made. In ancient times papyrus grew in profusion along the banks of the river and especially amid the swamps of the delta. The plant was just about all-purpose: the Egyptians lashed together bundles of the reeds to make canoes and rafts, laced them to make mats, baskets, boxes, and sandals, twisted the fibers to make cordage, and in times of a low Nile when food was scarce, ate the pith. The most important use by far, however, was in the manufacture of paper. Early in their career the Egyptians learned to slice the pith of the stalks longitudinally into thin strips, place these alongside each other in a double layer—one with the strips running up and down and the other with them running crosswise—pound with a mallet until all, thanks to the glutinous sap in the plant, were matted together in a single sheet, and polish the surface smooth with stone. The result was an excellent form of paper (our word "paper" derives from *papyros,* the Greek name of the plant), far cheaper than leather, far more practical than clay tablets. Egypt exported it all over, not only during ancient times but right up to the twelfth century A.D., when rag and wood-pulp paper finally began to displace it.

Farms were totally self-sufficient, growing and making their food and drink. "Make for me . . . grain into bread and beer," says a peasant to his wife as he leaves for a trip, "for every day in which I may be traveling." In other words, even a mere peasant farm, where the wife herself did the work about the house, milled its own flour, baked its own bread, and brewed its own beer. Large estates in addition spun and wove their own flax, extracted their own oil, even, as we shall see in a

moment, did their own slaughtering and butchering. They also produced enough of everything to supply the needs of the master's town
houses. Brewing, as it happens, required no special facility but was done
in the bakeshop, since its basic ingredient was partly baked loaves,
browned on the outside and raw in the middle. These were crumbled
into a vat along with water and trodden into a mash, which was carefully strained; the mixture was then poured into tall crocks to ferment
and when ready was decanted into jars that were carefully stoppered
with mud plaster.

Large estates were usually ranches as well as farms, raising sizable
herds of cattle. The temple foundations of Amon toward the end of the
New Kingdom owned more than four hundred thousand head. One of
the herds, in the eastern part of the delta, was so large that almost a
thousand men were needed to handle it. Cattle rustling seems to have
been as much a problem in ancient Egypt as in the American West, and
the same means were used to combat it—branding. The hands herded
the animals into a corner of a field, lassoed each in turn, rolled it onto its
back with its feet trussed, and branded it on the right shoulder—with
the inevitable scribe nearby to keep track of the inventory figures. Great
care and attention were given to fattening the herds, much more than
to the herdsmen; in one picture the artist, with typically sardonic Egyptian humor, shows a row of beefy cattle led by a herdsman so scrawny
that every bone in his body sticks out. Pictures and even wooden
models have been found in tombs showing the activities that went on at
the deceased's country estate, and a number illustrate how the cattle
were fed and slaughtered. One tomb yielded a model of a stall filled
with typical long-horned Egyptian cattle, red, black, and piebald; some
eat from a manger along the wall but others are being force-fed by
hand—including one that, too heavy to stand on its own legs, has fallen
on the floor, where a herdsman is cramming food into its mouth. An
accompanying model shows the estate slaughterhouse: butchers are
slitting the animals' throats with long knives while assistants catch the
blood in basins. As always, there are inspectors on hand to make sure no

choice cuts are spirited away, and scribes to keep inventory. From the rafters hang pieces of meat being cured. Among the butchers are some who are getting ready to dress and kill fowl.

Raising cattle was for the rich man. The poor kept goats and, in the delta area where the soil was moist enough, pigs. Sheep were of secondary importance. The ubiquitous beast of burden was the donkey. Horses were almost exclusively for the army, to pull chariots.

"The tenant-farmer, his reckonings go on forever . . ." wrote a supercilious member of the scribal class. "Wearier is he than a wayfarer of the delta. . . . His sides ache. . . . When he goes forth thence from the meadows and he reaches his home in the evening, he is one cut down by traveling." The Egyptian peasant may have worked less than a Greek, who had to coax crops out of a stony and scanty soil, but, as the scribe grimly observed, he still worked hard. Moreover, the Egyptian sun, though benign, is infernally hot, and the peasant could not set up comfortably under the shade of a tree, as supervisors and scribes did. Listen to his work songs, preserved for us in captions over the farming scenes that adorn the tombs:

a plowman sings,

> A good day—it is cool.
> The cattle are pulling,
> and the sky does according to our desire—
> Let us work for the noble!

the reapers sing,

> This good day is come forth in the land;
> the north wind is come forth,
> and the sky does according to our desire—
> let us work as our hearts may be bound!

and a herdsman driving cattle around a threshing floor sings,

> Thresh ye for yourselves, thresh ye for yourselves, O cattle!
> Thresh ye for yourselves, thresh ye for yourselves!

Straw to eat, and barley for your masters—
let not your hearts be weary, for it is cool.

Note the emphasis in all three—"it is cool."

He toiled in the heat, felt the foreman's stick, and unquestionably had to accept large doses of the proud man's contumely and the insolence of office, yet in one key respect the Egyptian peasant was better off than his brothers in the towns. When the Nile was low and food became scarce, they went hungry; we shall see later that empty bellies eventually drove the tomb workers of Ramses III to take the step, almost unheard of in the ancient world, of going out on strike. The peasant, even in the worst of times, was able to grub something to eat.

CHAPTER VI

At Leisure

The Valley of the Nile was a land of such bounteous plenty that under normal conditions it yielded enough not only to feed the population but to support a sizable upper crust of society in idleness. The beneficiaries—the royal family, the courtiers, the administrators, and other members of Egypt's elite—swiftly worked out ways and means of exploiting the situation: material ways and means, for the Egyptians were as material-minded as they were practical. They were the first, so far as we know, to develop the art of gracious living, the first to relish the joys of a comfortable and well-appointed home and of the activities that could be carried on in it.

The garden, for example, that we have noted as so essential a part of any dwelling, though it had its utilitarian side—it produced the household's fruits and vegetables—was primarily intended for the family's leisure moments. They strolled along the tree-lined paths, drifted over or paddled about the ponds, took meals alfresco in the pergolas. Indoors they whiled away the time chatting informally, listening to music, playing board games. Egyptian board games are the very earliest known; some specimens have been found in tombs of the First Dynasty, dating, in other words, between 3000 and 2800 B.C. As in Parcheesi or back-

A nobleman, accompanied by his wife and children, glides on a reed raft through a papyrus marsh hunting for fowl. (Painting in the tomb of Nakht at Thebes. Time of Thutmose IV.)

gammon, pieces were moved according to casts of the dice. During the New Kingdom the favorite game was *senet,* usually played with ten conical and spool-shaped pieces on a rectangular board divided into thirty squares. The boards were of wood adorned with ivory or ebony, the pieces of faience, wood, alabaster, or ivory. Archaeologists have recovered the paraphernalia for still more complicated games, including "hounds and jackals," played with ten pins serving as pieces, five, the "hounds," ending in lop-eared dogheads, and five, the "jackals," in pointed-eared dogheads; the board was oblong and, like a cribbage board, had rows of holes to receive the pins. Such games were by no means children's pastimes. The tomb pictures show adults playing them, often husband against wife; if a child is present in one of these scenes, it is only to stand alongside the father with an arm affectionately about his neck.

Much time was spent in lavish and gracious entertaining of guests—or so one would judge from the banquet scenes that occur in tomb after tomb, surely a reflection of the prominence these occasions had in life on earth. The host is usually shown greeting the guests at the gate and then leading them across the garden to the house, though some preferred to stand on their dignity and receive them against the impressive background of the reception hall, leaving it to the children or the servants to do the honors at the gate. There was always an exchange of formalities, ranging from lengthy invoking of blessings upon the arrivals to a simple "Welcome, welcome," or, getting right to the point, "Bread and beer."

The seating at dinner parties followed a regular pattern. Men and women were usually on opposite sides of the room, although married couples might be put together. The host and honored guests lolled in high-backed chairs, others made do with stools, and young girls squatted on cushions. All were garlanded, perfumed, and dressed in their best, with both men and women wearing make-up, bouffant wigs, rope upon rope of beads, and sheer linen garments. The emphasis was upon the groaning board—the guests faced tables piled high with quantities of meat, fowl, breads, vegetables, and fruits, and the beer and wine passed freely. One painting shows a servant holding out a cup of wine to a lady guest and saying to her, as the caption tells us, "Drink till thou art drunk! Spend thy day in happiness." The lady answers, "Give me eighteen measures of wine. Look—I love it madly!" Another nearby, awaiting her turn, cries, "Drink! Bottoms up! When is the cup coming round to me?" Some guests, male as well as female, went at the eating and drinking too long and too enthusiastically, and their neighbors at table had to hold their heads while they threw up or help them lie down. Only the host's intimates would dare let themselves go this way. Lesser lights had to watch their step. A collection of wise sayings, that is, standard Egyptian hardheaded hints on how to get along in life, advises that anyone who happens to be "one of those sitting at the table of one greater than thyself, take what he may give, when it is set before thy nose. Thou shouldst gaze at what is before thee. Do not pierce him with many stares (for such) an aggression against him is an abomination. . . . Let thy face be cast down until he addresses thee, and thou shouldst speak (only) when he addresses thee. Laugh after he laughs, and it will be very pleasing to his heart." Another word of caution, and this was for all guests, high as well as humble, was that in "any place where thou mightest enter, beware of approaching the women. It does not go well with the place where that is done. . . . A thousand men may be distracted from their (own) advantage. One is made a fool by limbs of faience, as she stands (there). . . . A mere trifle, the likeness of a dream— and one attains death through knowing her. . . . Do not do it—it is really an abomination." The collection was drawn up by Ptahhotep, a celebrated vizier who lived about 2400 B.C., but it remained forever popular, being copied and read right through New Kingdom times.

A proper party called for entertainment. There was always music— harps of all sizes, from a small portable type to the large standing harp, double and single flute, and a kind of lute with small box and very long neck that looks rather like a banjo. Often the musicians were girls. Usually there were dancing girls. Tomb pictures show pirouettes, backbends, splits, a chorus line of high kickers, an Egyptian *pas de deux,* and a dance in which the performer keeps her feet still, sinuously moving arms and hips—an ancient version of the Oriental shimmy. It was *comme il faut* to include songs praising the host's generosity. Other songs urged the guests to gather their rosebuds while they might, reminding them that all paths lead but to the grave and people take nothing with them there:

Follow thy desire, as long as thou shalt live.
Put myrrh upon thy head and clothing of fine linen upon thee,
being anointed with genuine marvels of the god's property.
Set an increase to thy good things;
let not thy heart flag.
Follow thy desire and thy good.
Fulfill thy needs upon earth, after the command of thy heart
until there comes for thee that day of mourning. . . .
REFRAIN: Make holiday and weary not therein!
Behold, it is not given to a man to take his property with him.
Behold, there is not one who departs who comes back again.

The song was first written about 2000 B.C. but, later generations agreeing with its message, it continued to be sung for centuries.

The Egyptian lord of the manor was a born sportsman, enjoying hunting and fowling—but not fishing, for that was a poor man's way of getting a kind of food that the upper classes did not eat. Fowling was carried on in the stands of papyrus reeds along the riverbanks or the dense thickets of them in the delta. The sportsman would glide about in a light reed skiff; often he took his wife and children with him, though not to participate, merely to have the fun of being spectators. A pet Nile goose might be aboard as decoy. The weapon was one that called for great skill—a boomerang. In the tomb pictures the huntsman never misses, boomerang and quarry neatly landing at his feet, where his children and wife grab them up. Some pictures show teams of men trapping whole flocks of birds in nets, but this presumably was for satisfying the needs of the master's larder rather than his taste for the joys of sport.

The hunting of animals took place in the desert, which was nowhere very far away. Here antelope, gazelles, wild cattle and donkeys, ostriches, and hares abounded. Most forays, to avoid the effort involved in running down such fleet-footed game, were conducted in deep-sided valleys, where, by the setting up of nets at strategic points, the quarry could be cornered. The hunters rode in chariots, equipped with bow and arrow and accompanied by dogs looking like our greyhounds. The

dogs ran the animals into the cul-de-sac, where the hunters cut them
down with a shower of arrows. A few hunters were sportsmanlike
enough to do it the hard way and run the game down in the open desert
until near enough to dispatch them with a shot.

Pharaohs were able to go in for big-game hunting in the course of
their wars in Syria or Nubia, where such animals were to be found.
Thutmose III, who extended Egypt's imperial boundaries deep into
Syria, while on campaign there conducted an elephant hunt that netted
him 120 beasts—"Never was the like done since the time of the god by a
king," he boasts in an inscription he set up, a copy of which has survived. Despite his assertion that he "said this without boasting therein,
and without equivocation therein," he omits mention of at least one
tight moment he had, which we happen to know from another inscription erected by a man in his escort: "He hunted 120 elephants at their
mudhole. Then the biggest elephant which was among them began to
fight before the face of His Majesty. I was the one who cut off his hand
[trunk] while he was (still) alive, in the presence of His Majesty, while
I was standing in the water between two rocks." His Majesty also
knocked off "seven lions by shooting in the completion of a moment,
and he captured a herd of twelve wild cattle within an hour."

Thutmose's son, Amenhotep II, was as passionate a Nimrod as his
father. He was such a crack shot—or so he claims in his inscriptions—
that he could send an arrow through a copper target three inches thick
with such force that nine inches stuck out behind. Once he set up four
such targets, each thirty-four feet from the other, took four arrows,
and, shooting from a fast-moving chariot, hit one after the other with
each "arrow coming out of it and falling to the ground"—in other
words, passing clean through. Amenhotep was one of the few who
scorned knocking off game like sitting ducks in a cul-de-sac and in-
sisted on running them down from a chariot; his horses were up to it
since he broke and trained them himself. Ramses III also claimed credit
for being a big-game hunter, and he had artists draw him going after
lions with javelin as well as bow and arrow. Perhaps the game was
brought down by arrows and dispatched with javelins.

Boys from noble families spent a good deal of time in various forms of athletics, particularly running and chariot driving, but these were as much training to develop their physical endurance as pastimes. The Greek writer Diodorus somewhere picked up the information that Ramses' father made him and his companions run twenty miles before breakfast. Amenhotep II, as enthusiastic for athletics as hunting, used to go to extraordinary lengths to get a workout. He would take over the stroke oar in the royal yacht and, as he tells us in an inscription, the rest of the crew of two hundred, after "they had attained half an *iter*'s course [less than two-thirds of a mile], they were weak, their bodies were limp, they could not draw a breath, whereas his majesty was strong under his oar of twenty cubits [34 feet] in its length. He left off and moored his boat only after he had attained three *iters* [ca. four miles] in rowing without letting down in pulling. Faces were bright at the sight of him when he did this."

Dallying in the garden or over the game board, giving or attending elaborate parties, fowling or hunting for the fun of it, rowing and other sports—all, as we have indicated, were only for the well-to-do. The poor man had to wait until one of the great annual festivals came around to enjoy leisure or be beguiled with entertainment. Every now and then, however, even he found a chance to take time out from work for a bit of fun. The men who manned the papyrus rafts that glided about the marshes used to indulge in horseplay, trying to knock each other off balance into the water. At times teams formed up for water jousting: two canoes, each with a team of paddlers and a man wielding a lance, squared off, and while the paddlers worked and maneuvered, the water-borne knights tried to upset one another.

The children, like children the world over, turned to play whenever they had the chance. The boys, as we would expect, went in for the rougher types of games. They had a version of tug-of-war in which the two columns of boys, instead of clutching a rope, clutched each other about the waist; those at the head of each column locked arms, and all pulled away with might and main. They played a version of leapfrog with the "frog" seated on the ground instead of bending over, since he was allowed to trip the leapers. They played ball, of course, and their balls, made of leather stuffed with barley chaff, were not very different from a modern indoor baseball, albeit much smaller. And in the tombs pieces of wood have been found whittled into a shape exactly like those used in our "cat," or tipcat, to give it its more formal name, the game in which a small stick with thinned ends is tipped by a bat so that it springs into the air and then is given a second blow to drive it horizontally. Girls also played ball—one painting shows a pair tossing a ball while riding piggyback—but their favored pastime was dancing. A group, in time-honored fashion, would form a circle and sing and clap as others whirled and pirouetted in the center.

CHAPTER VII

The Professions

Scribe and soldier—these were the ranking professions during all the centuries of ancient Egypt. And of them the first—at least according to the scribes—had pride of place. "Be a scribe," runs a writing exercise that all young apprentices to the art were made to copy as part of their training, "More effective is a book than a decorated tombstone. . . . A man is perished, his corpse is dust, all his relatives are come to the ground—(but) it is writing that makes him remembered. . . . More effective is a book than the house of the builder or tombs in the West. It is better than a (well-)founded castle or a stele in a temple."

Since Egypt was the source of all the ancient world's paper and Egyptians had an inborn taste for paperwork, and since, as we have seen, from their earliest days they were organized into a highly centralized state, the scribe was as pervasive in their society as the office worker in ours. Tomb pictures show him, squatting at the ready with papyrus scroll on knee and reed pen in hand—sometimes with extra pens stuck behind his ears just as our clerks do with pencils—in the fields to record the yield of the harvest, in the beer cellars to inventory the contents, in the slaughterhouses to list the cuts from the carcasses, in the army compounds to check the weapons issued, at trials to take down the proceedings. When Egyptian soldiers after a battle tossed into a heap hands cut from their slain enemies, there was the scribe to take a tally of the gory souvenirs. The pharaoh's tax system entered into the nation's every nook and cranny, and so did his scribes, to make sure that the farmer paid on his crops, the rancher on his herds, the artisan on his handiwork, even the fisherman on his catch and the hunter on his bag. Since coinage had not yet been invented, taxes were paid in produce and labor, which must have made the bookkeeping doubly complex.

Most of the scribes were in the service of the administrative arm of the government, working under the ultimate authority of the vizier, but there were sizable bodies employed by the armed forces and the religious foundations. Tallying enemy dead was the least of their services for the military; they took care of the mechanics of enlistment, kept the records for the commissary, the armory, and the other branches of supply, wrote dispatches—indeed, so ubiquitous were they that, in a tomb picture of a squad of sailors running at the double, each clutching a quarterstaff or an axe or a bow, right in their midst we see, keeping step, a scribe clutching his bundle of papyrus rolls and pen case. The temple estates of Amon, owning vast tracts of land and immense herds and housing and feeding hordes of priests, kept thousands of scribes busy.

Scribes had the white-collar worker's lofty contempt for those who earned a living by the sweat of their brow. Among the exercises the young apprentices in their schools were made to copy was one that smugly pointed out the profession's advantages over the gamut of humbler toilers, over the weaver, who "cannot breathe the open air" and who "if he cuts short the day of weaving . . . is beaten with fifty thongs"; the embalmer, whose "fingers are foul, for the odor thereof is of corpses"; the builder of walls, whose "sides ache since he must be outside in a treacherous wind"; the builder of houses, who "is dirtier than vines or pigs from treading under his mud," and so on. The document throws in as well some not so humble walks of life: a scribe is better off, it argues, than the courier, who goes out to a foreign country only "after he has made over his property to his children, being afraid of lions and Asiatics," or the merchant, who, once he has entered into "the Delta to get trade for himself . . . the gnats have slain him, the sand flies have made him miserably miserable."

But the document is discreetly quiet about the other side of the picture, the long and laborious training required to make a scribe, to teach him the complicated Egyptian system of writing. During the New Kingdom there were in general use about six hundred hieroglyphic signs; calligraphy, the forming of the signs and the setting them out in a pleasing pattern, was every bit as important as putting them together to make sense. An apprentice entered a school—the biggest were those run by the government to staff its administration, but there were others at the major religious foundations, and there may have been small private schools run by retired scribes. It is not likely that very many peasant children were in a position to undertake this demanding course of study; more likely it drew from the sons of middle-class fathers who were ambitious for their offspring and had the wherewithal to do something about it.

The schooling began quite early; we know of one scribe who enrolled at the age of five. The youngsters spent the next dozen years or so endlessly forming letters, memorizing, copying. One of their elementary textbooks has survived, bearing the sonorous title, "The teaching that maketh clever and instructeth the ignorant, the knowledge of all that existeth, what Ptah hath created and Thoth hath written, the heaven with its stars, the earth and what therein is, what the mountains disgorge, and what floweth forth from the ocean, concerning all things that the sun enlighteneth and all that groweth on the earth." What all this boils down to is nothing more than a collection of lists of words a government clerk might be expected to know, ranging from the names of the heavenly bodies to various kinds of food, including forty-eight different baked meats, twenty-four drinks, and thirty-three kinds of flesh.

From such lists the student advanced to copying classics of Egyptian literature, the precepts of certain revered sages of earlier times, or the famous *Hymn to the Nile*. He also was made to copy out model letters

Scribes of Ramses II tally the number of Hittites killed at the Battle of Qadesh (1300 B.C.) by counting a heap of hands severed from the corpses. (Relief in the Temple of Ramses II at Abydos.)

suitable for every conceivable occasion—including letters from schoolmasters chiding laggard pupils, and since, for form's sake, these were put in his own and his teacher's names, we find the boys urging one hundred lashes upon themselves for dissoluteness and laziness.

The boys did their practicing on flakes of stone, or potsherds, or wooden writing boards. Eventually, they graduated to using the excellent form of paper available, manufactured from strips of the papyrus reeds that grew in profusion along the banks of the river or in the marshes of the delta. They wrote on it with a reed pen dipped in water and rubbed over a cake of lampblack, just as we do with water colors.

It goes without saying that the schoolmasters considered the rod an indispensable teaching aid; as one of them put it, "a youngster's ear is in his back. He listens only to the man who beats him." None but a saint could have endured the monotonous grind without sometimes kicking over the traces, and Egyptians were no saints. The model letters the boys were made to copy out furnish lurid details. "I hear," an aggrieved master indites to a pupil, "that you are neglecting your writing and spending all your time dancing, going from tavern to tavern, always reeking of beer. . . . If only you realized that wine is a thing of the devil and could forget your wine jars! . . . You sit in the house with the girls around you. . . . You sit in front of the wench, sprinkled with perfume; your garland hangs around your neck and you drum on your paunch; you reel and fall on your belly and are filthied with dirt!"

But when a boy had finally completed his apprenticeship, the long years paid off well. Egypt could not do without its scribes; they were the equivalent of today's computer operators: they had mastered a complicated and arcane technique that was indispensable for the running of the government and the economy. Though not part of the ruling class, they worked in close association with it, and this meant that, at the very least, their standard of living was raised from the middle-class level of their birth to one more consonant with the palace or temple precincts where they took up residence. For those who were gifted and ambitious, the profession opened the doors to advancement, offering one of the few ways available for climbing the rungs of the social ladder. As early as the Fifth Dynasty men were taking advantage of the situation. A certain Uni rose from a mere keeper of a warehouse through a succession of offices to become governor of Upper Egypt. Then there was Nekhebu, who advanced from "common builder" to Royal Constructor and Architect. In a surviving inscription he tells us how he did it:

When I accompanied my brother, the Foreman of Construction Work . . . I acted as clerk, I carried the scribe's palette. When he was appointed journeyman builder, I carried his measuring rod. When he was appointed master builder, I accompanied him. When he was appointed Royal Constructor and Builder, I ruled the (workman's) city for him. I did everything thoroughly in it. . . . As for everybody there with whom I had to negotiate, it was I who made them satisfied, and I never went to bed angry against anybody.

The most spectacular case in point is Amenhotep-son-of-Hapu, who, born of a father in a modest position, advanced by way of the army's corps of scribes to become the right-hand man of Pharaoh Amenhotep III. His official titles were Chief Recruiting Officer and Overseer of Public Works. In the first capacity he arranged for important troop and naval dispositions on both sides of the delta, in the second for the transport of the two huge statues of Amenhotep III that still stand near Thebes.

The pharaoh was so grateful for the various services rendered by his efficient subordinate that he allowed him to erect in the temple at Karnak several statues of himself; we see him in the traditional posture of a royal scribe, squatting with a scroll on his lap. Even more striking, the pharaoh granted him permission to build a mortuary temple of monumental size next to the royal temples in western Thebes; no other man of modest birth had ever before been so honored. Amenhotep III endowed his favorite's temple in perpetuity; services in his name were carried on there long after his death, and a cult grew up around this most successful of scribes. He came to be revered as one of Egypt's great sages, and proverbs attributed to him were translated into Greek twelve centuries after his time.

Scribes were among the few who had opportunities to travel: since bookkeeping was needed just as much in Egypt's foreign possessions as in the homeland, many put in a tour of duty in Syria or Palestine; in Egypt itself, as we shall see later, they were indefatigable tourists. There were opportunities for graft. A document has been found, dating from near the end of the New Kingdom, which tells of a riverboat captain who embezzled more than 90 per cent of the grain he contracted to deliver to a certain temple over a period of nine years; clearly he could not have gotten away with such grand larceny without buying the silence not only of the scribes who booked in the grain at the temple but of all the others involved in the transaction from the moment the grain left the farmers' fields. And, failing all else, as *petits fonctionnaires* scribes were always able to lord it over Egypt's humble and gratify the self-importance that had been drummed into them at school.

The Soldier

The scribe's self-importance was such that he looked down, or affected to look down, on the soldier. The exercises that detail the miseries of other callings reach a crescendo when setting forth those of the soldier: "He carries his bread and his water on his shoulders like an ass' burden; his spine is dislocated; he drinks brackish water and sleeps with one eye open. . . . When the time comes for him to return to Egypt he is like a worm-eaten piece of wood. He is ill, paralysis seizes him, and he has to be led on a donkey." The schoolmasters had to lay it on thick; many of their young charges, copying some interminable list for the hundredth time, would no doubt happily have chucked it all for the joys of prancing about a barracks yard. And in the days of the empire, when the needs of war and garrisoning called forth an ever larger military establishment, wielding a bow or javelin offered as much chance for money and preferment as wielding a pen.

The Egyptians, though their art is full of scenes of gory battle and their annals of bloody triumphs, were not particularly good soldiers, and they were long protected more by their desert barriers than by the valor of their arms. All during Old Kingdom and Middle Kingdom times there was no standing army, except for a small cadre of troops about the pharaoh. When there was an emergency he mustered a sort of feudal levy of men by calling upon the provincial nobles, who thereupon conscripted the local peasants. The motley force, under the command of a royal son or some high noble, went off to meet the threat; when it was over, the men were disbanded and they returned to their mattocks and plows. Toward the end of the Old Kingdom the practice arose of adding some stiffening in the form of foreign troops, either captives or volunteers enticed into the service. These were mostly black tribesmen from the Sudan with some Berbers from Libya, both of whom had a taste for war.

The Egyptians, on top of being no more than casual recruits, were poorly equipped. They went into battle without helmet or body armor, protected only by a bull's-hide shield, in some cases a handy buckler but in others a full-length affair that was heavy and clumsy. Their chief weapon was the bow, a type made of a single piece of wood that was not particularly powerful. Next in importance to the archers were the spearmen, wielding either short javelins or long spears, the height of a man, with a copper tip.

The Hyksos, whose arrival from Palestine and Syria brought the Middle Kingdom to a close, brutally revealed to the Egyptians how far behind they were. They wore helmets and body armor, used the strong Asiatic bow—made of wood, sinew, and horn glued together—and carried the Syrian scimitar, an effective curved sword. Above all, they had a chariot corps. By this time the horse was in common use in many parts of the Near East, and the horse-drawn chariot had become to ancient armies what the tank is to modern. It took Egypt almost two centuries to learn to use the invader's weapons and wield them against him.

Shortly after 1500, under Thutmose III, Egypt turned the tables and, as we have seen, became an invader herself, moving north into Palestine and Syria and south deeper into the Sudan than she had ever penetrated before and welding both areas into a loosely controlled empire. A proper military establishment had come into being, consisting of volunteers, conscripts, and foreign units. All were armed with the newest and best weapons available: helmet, leather jerkin covered with scales of metal, shield, javelin, Asiatic bow. Archers and spearmen were organized into platoons of 50 men each, platoons into companies of 200 (later 250), and companies into divisions of 5,000. The pride of the army was the chariot corps, arranged in squadrons of 25 chariots each. The chariots, designed for speed and maneuverability, were extremely light, being made of light wood bound by leather thongs. Each was manned by a driver and an archer, a youth from the upper classes; the chariotry was an elite corps. An elaborate supply organization backed up the fighting units, assuring them spare weapons and food (bread, cake, beef, vegetables, wine) in abundance. The supply units included cooks, bakers, donkey drivers (transport was done on donkeyback), and, of course, scribes. The army also had a naval arm, a fleet of galleys of light build intended primarily for use on the river.

Nubian archers with bows and arrows march alongside Egyptian soldiers with lances and shields. (Model found in a tomb of Middle Kingdom date, now in the Cairo Museum.)

We remarked above that as early as the end of the Old Kingdom there were Sudanese troops in Egypt's armies. Many were settled up and down the land to serve as a police force—on such a scale that, by New Kingdom times, the word *Medjai,* meaning Sudanese warriors, came to be the regular term for police. The Sudanese were in time joined by other foreigners—Hittites, Syrians, above all, Libyans. From 1300 B.C. on, Libyan Berbers began entering in ever-increasing numbers until, within a century, they made up by themselves the bulk of the armed forces, like the Goths in the armies of the later Roman Empire. Inevitably they ended up putting their own commanders on the throne: from about 950 to 724 Egypt was ruled by Libyan pharaohs.

The soldiers, both native and foreign, came to form a distinct class, powerful and well-to-do. In addition to their pay and their share of

whatever booty was taken, they were given allotments of land in communities that gradually grew to be veritable military colonies. The foreigners became thoroughly Egyptianized in their dress and way of life. Yet, so far as we can tell, no integration took place. Reliefs dating near the end of the period that interests us, about 1200 B.C., include, complete with captions, pictures of wrestling and other contests between Egyptians and Sudanese or Libyans; the captions are full of ethnic slurs, and in every case the Egyptian triumphs. In one scene the referee, an Egyptian, with blatant partiality shouts encouragement to his compatriot.

The army, like the corps of scribes, offered a chance for getting ahead. A foot soldier could rise to lead a platoon or company. Officers were rewarded for gallantry in action with gifts of gold, slaves, and land.

Some were given lucrative government posts at retirement, such as chief of police or chief steward on a royal estate. And the highest officers found themselves in a position to go after the highest prize, the throne. In the earliest days of the New Kingdom the pharaoh himself acted as commander in chief. Later he turned the job over to the crown prince. By Akhenaten's time, it was being filled by a professional soldier, Horemheb, who was able to use his post as a steppingstone to the royal power, a move that was repeated by his successor, Ramses I.

The Medical Profession

The doctors of Egypt, asserted Homer, "are skilled beyond all men." During New Kingdom times the rulers of Egypt's neighbors used to importune the pharaohs for the services of Egyptian physicians. Centuries later Cyrus, founder of the Persian Empire, kept a number at his court and so did Darius, Persia's greatest king; they were still considered the best in the world in the sixth century B.C.

The medical profession, like so many aspects of Egyptian life, was organized and supervised. There were administrators who bore titles such as "overseer of doctors," "inspector of doctors," "chief of doctors." There may even have been an organized group of women doctors, for an inscription, dating from Old Kingdom times, records a person with a woman's name who has a title that seems to mean "overseer of the female doctors." There is some uncertainty about the translation, but, if correct, it points to the presence of women doctors in ancient Egypt, millenniums before their next appearance in history.

The upper crust of the profession was formed by the "doctors of the palace," i.e., those who served the nobles of the court. They too were organized and supervised: there was a "chief of the doctors of the palace," an "overseer of the doctors of the palace," an "inspector of the doctors of the palace." At the very top of the profession were the men charged with the care of the pharaoh and his family, the "doctor of the lord of the two lands," "the doctor to the queen," and similar titles. Even they were organized and supervised, for the preserved titles include a "chief of doctors to the lord of the two lands" and an "inspector of doctors to the king."

Some Egyptian doctors were general practitioners, some were specialists; in Herodotus' day the latter were so numerous that he was led to believe that all Egyptian doctors were specialists. As it happens, specialization is characteristic of the most primitive forms of medicine as well as the most advanced; the medicine man frequently limits his practice to certain areas or ailments. There are examples of Egyptian doctors who specialized from as early as Old Kingdom times. One of the doctors of the palace, Irenakhty, boasted an expertise that took in both ends of the body: he was not only court ophthalmologist but also court proctologist (literally "herdsman of the anus"). There were doctors who practiced dentistry as well as medicine and some who were solely dentists. There must have been veterinarians, for among the surviving Egyptian medical writings is a treatise on veterinary medicine. And the army doubtless had a medical corps specially trained to handle battle injuries.

Just as a would-be doctor today starts with a general education and moves on from there to medicine, his Egyptian counterpart began by enrolling in a school for scribes and learning to read and write fluently. Little information is available about medical training. No doubt many got it through apprenticeship; there are instances of sons following fathers into the profession and in these cases the sons surely learned through apprenticeship. Certain temples may have offered training, since cure by prayers and spells, as we shall see in a moment, was to the Egyptian as legitimate a form of medicine as any we hold by today. But, as we can tell from the Edwin Smith Papyrus and the Ebers Papyrus, there was also solid training in empirical-rational practice including surgery; indeed, these writings or others like them might well have served as textbooks. That a would-be doctor had to be literate and have extensive training in effect closed the door of the profession to all but upper-class youths. In fact, a statue of a palace doctor, who was in charge of some facility involving medical students, bears an inscription that states he chose the "students from among sons of men of consequence, no sons of the poor were among them."

The crowning achievement of a doctor's career was to gain a post at the palace, as a member of the team that guarded the health of the pharaoh, his family, and the court. The royal physicians even had a boat at their disposal to enable them to get without delay to wherever they might be needed. Next in preference was a post as household doctor to members of the nobility. Such an assignment assured a man board and lodging of the best as well as a chance to earn rich gifts. Well below such a post in desirability were the jobs as resident physician at state institutions and enterprises such as the mines, quarries, and various building projects. Lastly, there were the doctors attached to the temples, who, in addition to treating the temple personnel, probably took care of the general public roundabout. Medical services, thus, were to a considerable extent free: anyone connected with the palace, rich or poor, was treated by one of the palace staff, anyone with a noble's household by the physician in residence, others by the temple physicians.

When we read the medical writings preserved from ancient Egypt, we greet with wonder and admiration the physicians' striking achievements in what we consider true medicine and shake our heads mournfully over the prayers and charms and spells that share the same pages. We must, however, look at the matter through an Egyptian's eyes. From the point of view of his understanding of disease, both types of treatment were equally "scientific," and, indeed, the magical-religious had definite advantages. Employing that most powerful of curing agents, psychological suggestion, it enjoyed a certain measure of success, was cheaper, and, most important of all, could be called upon in cases where rational treatment manifestly could not—a recommendation that has guaranteed its existence to this very day.

When people fell sick, it was believed that they somehow had either incurred the wrath of a god or been unfortunate enough to have an evil spirit enter their bodies. Only in disabilities such as battle wounds or physical injuries did the matter rest clearly within the realm of medicine as we know it. Thus Egypt's medical profession consisted of priests and magicians as well as doctors. If you suffered a cut you went to a doctor. If you had a bellyache, you might still go to him—though if you were convinced that the cause was a god's anger you would first hasten to a priest for the appropriate prayer, or if you thought a demon had attacked you, to a magician for the ritual of exorcism. Doubtless there were many who tried all three in hopes of assuring a cure.

Spirits were believed to behave like humans, so the magician used on them the same techniques we use on each other—curses, threats, warnings, orders, entreaties. Here is an example of a threat: "O ghost, male or female, thou hidden, thou concealed one, who dwelleth in this my flesh, in these my limbs—get thee hence from this my flesh, from these my limbs. Lo, I bring thee excrements to devour! Beware, hidden one, be on your guard, concealed one, escape!" The exact words had to be uttered, accompanied by exact execution of prescribed gestures; the slightest mistake or omission destroyed the efficacy of the spell. Often the exorcism was accompanied by the eating of some vile concoction, one guaranteed to turn the stomach even of a demon and drive him to seek a more appetizing menu elsewhere. If the spell or charm did not work immediately, the magician prepared a talisman or amulet, which would extend the effects for as long as it was worn. This might be no more than a band of linen over which the magical words had been spoken or upon which they were written. Or it might be something much more complicated and expensive, such as a necklace of beads made from precious or semiprecious stones. Often the amulet included a knotted cord, since knots were thought to have the ability to bind forces or present obstacles. Often it was impregnated with garlic or other strong-smelling substances that any fastidious ghost could be expected to stay away from. Often the evil stuff was consumed—always, to be sure, with the fitting incantations—to become an internal amulet exercising its expulsive power from inside. Perhaps it was in this way that proper pharmacy arose. Certain ingredients of the magical concoctions would have a manifest pharmacological effect, which doctors would eventually come to notice and remember—that, for example, castor oil caused a movement of the bowels. True medicine was born the moment that a doctor prescribed a given concoction without an accompanying charm or spell. In some of the Egyptian medical writings that have been preserved they are so given, but by no means in all. In practice they very likely were usually accompanied by incantation, since Egyptian doctors would want the magical benefits of the drugs they prescribed as well as the pharmaceutical.

Egypt's materia medica included vegetable, animal, and, to a lesser extent, mineral substances. Most could be found in any garden or barnyard; some were exotic imports, and the concoctions that called for them doubtless were intended for the upper-class clientele. A good many, if not the majority, of the ingredients in Egyptian prescriptions could have had only a psychological effect. This was certainly true of the many examples recorded of *Dreckapotheke,* demon-discouraging mixtures involving excrement, a type of recipe found in all civilizations and still popular in folk medicine. Psychological effect, of course, is not to be underrated; think how often we feel better the minute we have swallowed the pills our doctors have given us. But ingredients such as castor oil or dates or figs, with their laxative effect, or honey with its beneficial effect on wounds, must have been genuinely useful to ancient Egyptian patients; they still have a place in modern pharmacopoeias.

In 1862 one of the pioneers of American Egyptology, Edwin Smith, purchased a long papyrus from a dealer in Luxor. The document was a monograph on various kinds of wounds, presenting in clear and organized fashion how a doctor was to go about treating them. Although the papyrus itself dates from the first half of the sixteenth century B.C., it unquestionably is based on writings that are much older, that go back to at least Middle Kingdom and perhaps Old Kingdom times. A total of forty-eight surgical cases are discussed, arranged from head to foot, that is, starting with wounds in the head and proceeding through the throat, neck, shoulders, to the spine. Each is dealt with in the same fashion. First there is a title, derived from the chief symptom, for example, "Instructions for a gaping wound in his head, penetrating to the bone, and splitting his skull." Then follows the examination. This involves, just as today, interrogation, palpation, and functional tests. Then follows the diagnosis, usually a repetition of the words in the title: the doctor is instructed that he "shouldst say concerning him [the patient] 'one having a gaping wound, etc.' " Lastly there is the verdict, one of three possibilities: (1) "an ailment which I will treat," (2) "an ailment with which I will contend," (3) "an ailment not to be treated," or, as we would put it, favorable, uncertain, unfavorable. The view that a physician was not to treat hopeless cases was standard in the ancient world. Any alleviation was left to the priest or the magician.

The nature of the material has led to the suggestion that the Edwin Smith Papyrus was drawn up for use by army surgeons. Another important medical papyrus, called the Ebers Papyrus after the German Egyptologist Georg Ebers, is much longer than the Edwin Smith Papyrus and was evidently intended for the general practitioner. It includes the treatment of internal diseases; prescriptions for diseases of the eye (which obviously plagued the ancient Egyptian as much as the modern), of the skin, and of the extremities; miscellaneous prescriptions; gynecology; two treatises on the heart and its vessels; ailments requiring surgery and their treatment.

The last rubric includes cases that are discussed somewhat in the manner of the Edwin Smith Papyrus, with title, examination, diagnosis, verdict, and treatment. The other rubrics necessarily are different, being for the most part a listing of recipes, charms, and spells. This is precisely what we might expect: a dislocated jaw cannot be reduced by a spell, but there were many internal diseases against which spells or charms or magical concoctions were just about the only recourse an Egyptian doctor had. To its credit the Ebers Papyrus most often prescribes recipes without any hocus-pocus. In only a dozen cases, obviously considered all but hopeless, are incantations alone prescribed.

The two papyri reveal how an Egyptian doctor went about his business—and it is clear that his methods were not too different from those in use today. He started by interrogating the patient, learning that he was "too oppressed to eat" or that "all his limbs" were "heavy for him" or that he had "pains in both his sides," and so on. All the time he subjected him to keen scrutiny, noting whether he was pale or ruddy, whether his eyes were bloodshot or burning or had white spots, and the like. The descriptions preserved reveal the care with which the Egyptian doctor did his observing: a patient was said to be "weak like a breath that passes away" or have "it on his back like the trouble of one who has been stung" or have a face that looks "as if he had wept." The doctor took specimens as well, of the urine, feces, and "what is lifted by cough." Here too his descriptions have a nice exactness; blood after an intestinal hemorrhage is said to be "like pig's blood after it is fried." In addition to interrogation and observation, just as doctors do today, he palpated his patients. The Edwin Smith Papyrus instructs him to probe a wound to find out how deep it is and whether the skull is broken. In one case palpation revealed "a very large swelling protruding on his breast, oily, like fluid under thy hand." Palpation of a cystoid swelling revealed that it "goes and comes under thy fingers and it is as separated things by thy hand when it is fixed." The doctor felt various parts of a patient's body to determine temperature; the writings often mention the presence of fever. He felt the pulse—not to count it, but as an indication of general bodily condition; "His heart beats feebly" was recognized as an alarming symptom.

The Egyptian doctor was at his best with wounds. Cuts were treated by applying a piece of fresh meat—a very sensible procedure, since the meat acted as a cushion and thus stopped hemorrhage by means of pressure. Or he cauterized, or applied poultices of honey, oil, and other ingredients. If a wound was wide open, he brought it together with a form of adhesive plaster, "two . . . bandages of linen which are applied to the two lips of a gaping wound to cause one to be joined to the other." He also used suturing. Fractures he bound in splints of pieces of wood wrapped with linen bandaging. There is no question of his ability in this area; of the skeletons that have been examined, there are hundreds that show fractures which healed successfully. He was even able to achieve something in dentistry. Two instances have been unearthed of prosthetic dentistry, teeth fastened together with fine gold wire, a loose one to a sound one. Since so few examples have turned up, the practice could not have been widespread. Probably it was reserved only for the very rich.

For disease, the gamut of human ailments that have no obvious cause, the Egyptian doctor's chief remedy was pharmacotherapy. The present-day distinction between pharmacist and doctor did not exist then; the physician compounded his own prescriptions. He boiled them, strained them, and pounded them in stone mortars, carefully measuring the ingredients. Internal remedies were generally in liquid form, the vehicles being water, beer, wine, or milk. Sometimes they were made into a candy with honey, sometimes into pills of bread dough. External prescriptions included ointments made with olive, castor, or other oils, and salves of animal grease. All were generally quite complicated. For example, the recipe for an astringent salve for topical application in cases of a prolapsed rectum as given in the Ebers Papyrus runs as follows: "For a dislocation in the hinder part: myrrh, frankincense, rush-nut from the garden, *mhtt* from the shore, celery, coriander, oil, salt, are boiled together, applied in seed wool and put in the hinder part."

Just as Egypt's doctors became the most famous in the ancient world and held that reputation throughout ancient times, so too did the pharmaceutical prescriptions they compounded. The materia medica that we find in the works of the Greco-Roman doctor Galen, who so influenced later medicine, or in those of Dioscorides, the learned Greek whose *De Materia Medica* was used from the first to the sixteenth century A.D., undoubtedly drew upon Egyptian sources. What Egyptian doctors prescribed in Old Kingdom times lived on to serve patients for the next three millenniums and more, the good and the bad, those with no more pharmaceutical effect than our sugar-coated pills and those that contained such genuinely useful ingredients as castor oil, storax, and aloe. Some of their prescriptions have survived the centuries practically unchanged. For a couple anxious to know whether they will have a boy or girl, an Egyptian papyrus advises to put wheat and barley into separate containers, add the pregnant woman's urine, and "if the barley grows, it means a male, if the wheat grows, it means a female." Over two millenniums later, people are still being advised to try precisely the same procedure.

Engineers

Cheops [wrote Herodotus] . . . put all the Egyptians to work for him. At his orders men took blocks from the quarries in the hills on the east bank and dragged them to the Nile; they were ferried across the river, where others took them and hauled them to the hills on the west bank. The work was carried on throughout the year in three-month shifts of 100,000 men each. The time needed for the laboring masses to lay the causeway up which the stone was hauled was ten years; with a length of about 980 yards, a width of 20, and rising 16 yards at its highest point, built of polished stone carved with figures of animals, it is no less a feat, in my opinion, than the pyramid itself. The ten years included the buildings on the mound where the pyramid stands, the underground chambers, and the vaults Cheops built for himself on an island formed by cutting a canal to the Nile.

The time needed for the building of the pyramid itself was twenty years. It is square, with each face measuring 800 feet along the base and the same in height, of polished stone superbly fitted. None of the blocks are less than 30 feet. The way the pyramid was built was in tiers—battlement-wise, as some put it, altar-wise as others. When one such tier had been completed, blocks for the next were lifted by means of devices made of short lengths of wood. First they raised blocks from the ground to the top of the first tier. Then, to get blocks on top of this, they used another device set on top of the first tier, yet another to take it from there to the next. . . .

There is an inscription in Egyptian characters on the pyramid about how much was expended for radishes, onions, and garlic for the workers. I distinctly remember that the interpreter who read it to me said the cost was 1,600 talents of silver. If this is so, how much can we assume was paid for the rest, for tools for the work and meals and clothing for the men?

Herodotus, who saw the pyramids about the middle of the fifth century B.C., was shown about by a tourist guide, who was responsible for the balderdash about the astronomical cost merely for seasoning the men's food; the guides of that age could no more read Old Kingdom hieroglyphs than Herodotus could. It was probably from him that Herodotus got the figure for the size of the work gangs—which may be less nonsensical. Herodotus, however, as he tells us later, did his own measuring of the base, and his figure of eight hundred feet is very close to that reached by archaeologists (755 feet). The building, no question about it, was a marvel of engineering.

What is more, it was accomplished with the most primitive of tools. The better than two million blocks that make it up, averaging two and one half tons with some as big as ten tons, were quarried and cut by means of stone and copper tools. Since the block and tackle were not known in Egypt, the blocks could not have been lifted and dropped in place; each was painfully moved about on sleds or rollers, hauled up sloping ramps that led to the level being worked and that rose as the pyramid rose, and levered into position with poles.

One of the engineers' greatest feats was the smoothing off of the part of the plateau where the pyramid stands into an absolutely square and level area for its base. This may have been done by creating an artificial watercourse, its sides built up with mud, all around the area. The water set a level line, and by measuring down from it, the engineers could tell the diggers and pickmen how much had to be cut away to leave a perfectly flat square for the base—which may explain why Herodotus talks of cutting a canal from the Nile and transforming part of the complex into an island.

The great pyramids built during the Old Kingdom are the most notable of Egypt's engineering achievements, but they are by no means the only ones. The colossal 50-foot statues of Amenhotep III, the Hypostyle Hall at Karnak built by Seti I and Ramses II with its forest of 134 columns each 33 feet around and 69 to 75 feet high, the temple of Ramses II at Abu Simbel with its façade decorated by four 67-foot statues of the pharaoh—these and numerous other New Kingdom structures were tremendous feats. Yet, during the whole period of Egyptian engineering, from the first stone building put up by Imhotep about 2650 B.C. to Ramses' Brobdingnagian structures fifteen hundred years later, the same primitive tools and methods were used.

No less rudimentary than the technology were the means of reckoning and measuring and figuring that the architects employed in designing the structures and the engineers in working up the specifications.

The Egyptians knew no higher mathematics, just arithmetic so simple that it involved only addition and subtraction; they made these do the work that we perform by multiplying or dividing. To multiply, say, 23 by 13 they doubled and redoubled the multiplicand, as follows,

$$\star\ 1 \times 23 = 23 \qquad \star\ 4 \times 23 = 92$$
$$2 \times 23 = 46 \qquad \star\ 8 \times 23 = 184$$

continuing to do so until they had as many doublings as would add up to 13 (8 + 4 + 1; the numbers starred). Then they added the corresponding numbers on the right (184 + 92 +23) to arrive at the result, 299.

They used a similar system for dividing. To divide, say, 49 by 8 they doubled the divisor,

$$1 \times 8 = 8 \qquad \star\ 4 \times 8 = 32$$
$$\star\ 2 \times 8 = 16 \qquad 8 \times 8 = 64$$

then, by trial and error, they determined that the doublings 4 + 2 added up to 48, the number closest to the figure to be divided, and thus arrived at the answer of 6⅛. Fractions were one of the clumsiest features of their arithmetical computation, since they used only unit fractions, fractions with a numerator of one. What we express so conveniently today with the figure ¹³⁄₁₆, they expressed as ½ + ¼ + ¹⁄₁₆. Somehow or other Egypt's planners, by means of these primitive procedures, were able to make the calculations required to measure off the areas where they placed their structures, plot the positions of corridors and internal chambers and prescribe what extra bracing these would require, estimate the amounts of materials needed, handle the logistics involved in housing and feeding the gangs and apportioning the work among them, and so on.

The first Egyptian architect known by name is Imhotep, who built for Pharaoh Djoser of the Third Dynasty the famous Step Pyramid that still stands near Memphis. Imhotep filled at the same time any number of other high offices, and, as it happens, so did all the other so-called chief architects whose names turn up in Egyptian records. For Senmut,

Hatshepsut's official-of-all-trades, Chief Architect was only one of the multitudinous hats he wore. These court favorites, it would appear, were not the actual builders but rather ministers in charge of the branch of government involved.

The men who did the calculations, drew up the plans, surveyed the sites, and supervised the work day to day probably bore only that all-purpose Egyptian title, scribe. It brought a certain social standing but not enough to ensure, save for a few exceptions, the recording of their names. Equally unknown are the painters who so finely decorated the walls of Egypt's buildings and tombs, the sculptors who carved the splendid statues that went into them, the cabinetworkers who fashioned the handsome furniture and other fittings. To these humble but supremely gifted people we now turn.

VIII

Fine Craftsmen

Egypt's craftsmen, though working with the most primitive tools, turned out products of exquisite workmanship and beauty. The most striking manifestation of their skill occurs very early, in the fourth millennium B.C., reaching its zenith just after 3000. They developed at this early date the art of carving vases out of stone, achieving results unmatched anywhere else then or since. In a bravura display of their ability they did not limit themselves to limestone or alabaster or other soft rocks but chose the hardest there are—diorite, dolerite, basalt, granite. Somehow they learned to work this intractable material using copper and stone tools.

They first fashioned the outside of a vase, probably by pounding with a stone ball or by delivering jarring strokes with a blunt copper pick; a blow with just the proper amount of force from such an instrument will succeed in knocking off pieces from much harder substances. The next problem, the scooping out of the interior, must have been done with the aid of some abrasive, such as quartz sand, which is harder than most stone and will abrade even stone of the same hardness, just as diamond dust will cut diamonds. Vases that were cylindrical could be scooped out by endless drilling, with the bit turning in wetted fine quartz sand, the sand doing the actual cutting. The craftsmen's skill was so accomplished that they were able to leave the walls of a vase paper-thin, no more than a millimeter in thickness. But what of the narrow-necked vases? How were they able to scoop them out? We can only conclude that, by manipulating with infinite patience their tools through the narrow opening, they succeeded in drilling and chiseling out under the shoulders.

Another skill that the Egyptians developed precociously was in carpentry and cabinetwork. Its start was necessarily delayed until the manufacture of copper tools, which did not take place until the end of the fourth millennium B.C., but immediately thereafter the craft forged ahead with astonishing rapidity. In the tombs of First Dynasty kings has been found furniture whose workmanship was hardly to be surpassed in quality throughout the rest of Egyptian history. Since trees are scarce in Egypt and those that are there, such as acacia, yield only short lengths, the cabinetworkers swiftly became masters of the art of joinery, using with assurance pegs, dowels, mortises and tenons, dovetails, half-laps, and other joints. They learned to inlay with ivory or faience or exotic woods such as ebony, to veneer, and to fashion plywood with as many as six layers.

It was all achieved with simple copper, later bronze, tools. Rough hewing was done with axes, the cutting of planks with saws; by the set of the teeth we can tell that the cut was made on the pull and not the push as with today's type. They had a variety of chisels, heavy for rough work and fine for delicate work, some with handles rounded at the top that were manipulated by hand alone, some with flat-topped handles that were pounded by a hammer. Hammers were of wood, shaped rather like short clubs. Prominent among their tools was the awl for piercing holes; very likely used in connection with a bow, it served for drilling. The one tool they lacked was the plane, which did not make its appearance until the beginning of the Christian era. They used instead the adze, even as their descendants do today, made of a metal blade bound by a leather thong to a wooden handle. They wielded this primitive instrument with a dexterity that produced surfaces as smooth and straight as any our carpenters achieve with the plane. Inlays were fastened, and pieces of wood were cemented together, with strong glues derived from boiling skin, bone, and cartilage in water. In New Kingdom times, when the craftsmen were called upon to build chariots, they learned to bend wood by heat for the fellies of the wheels and the curved railings.

Weaving is an art that develops early in most cultures, and Egypt was no exception. As we have already observed, flax rather than wool was the preferred fiber (cotton, an exotic import from India throughout ancient times, was never in common use), and by the First Dynasty Egyptian weavers were turning out linen textiles as fine as any of today, with 160 threads to the inch in the warp and 120 in the woof. Though vegetable dyes were known, garments were usually left the color of the raw linen, as we can tell from the many representations in Egyptian paintings. Among other advantages, it made washing easier.

Poor Egyptians went around barefoot or in sandals made of plaited reeds, those who could afford it in sandals of leather. Tanning was yet another craft that arose early in the Valley of the Nile. The ample flocks of cattle, sheep, and goats provided abundant hides; gazelle skin was also occasionally used. Footwear was only one of a number of everyday objects fashioned from leather. The Egyptians made bags out of it, quivers for their arrows, seats for their chairs, mattresses for their beds, tent covers, and thongs for a variety of purposes. Adze blades, which had to fit as tightly as possible were bound to the handle with wetted thongs. Chariots, which had to be as light as possible, were given floors of interlaced leather straps.

Until the Middle Kingdom, when bronze came into use, smiths perforce made do with copper, fashioning it into tools, weapons, utensils, ornaments, and, eventually, statuary. The Sinai was the earliest source of supply; considerable remains of mining sites have been found there, though not all were for the extraction of copper, since turquoise was also mined in the peninsula. In New Kingdom times, when Egypt was in regular commercial contact with western Asia, the pharaohs imported abundant amounts of copper from Syria, which in turn had imported it from the rich deposits in Cyprus. The Sinai is separated from the Nile Valley by a stretch of desert, and the journey across it was hard on all concerned, not only the porters and pack donkeys but even the officials, as we can tell from an eloquent inscription left by the pharaoh's seal-bearer, who had to make the punishing trip sometime around 1810 B.C.:

This land was reached in the third month of the second season, although it was not at all the season for coming to this mining area [indeed it was not; the time was close to the beginning of June]. This seal-bearer . . . says to the officials who may come to this mining area at this season: Let not your faces flag because of it . . . I came from Egypt with my face flagging. It was difficult, in my experience, to find the skin for it, when the land was burning hot, the highland was in summer, and the mountains branded a blistered skin.

The copper was transported to the shops in Egypt, where it was worked either by hammering or casting. Handles and spouts for jugs were attached with copper rivets. A copper jug discovered a few decades ago reveals that as early as 2700 B.C. Egyptian craftsmen were able to draw copper wire, for the jug's handle, looped over the top, is bound to the neck by wire. One of the most remarkable feats of Egyptian metalworkers is a life-sized statue of Pharaoh Pepi I (about 2300 B.C.) made of pieces of hammered copper riveted together over a core of wood.

During the Middle Kingdom a transition took place: copper gradually bowed out in favor of bronze. Very likely the change was hastened by the appearance on the scene of the Hyksos with their powerful bronze daggers and swords. Bronze, an alloy of copper with some 3 to 16 per cent of tin, has the advantage of being harder, having a lower melting point, and flowing better when heated in crucibles for casting. Though copper was relatively plentiful in the Mediterranean area, tin was not. In later ages supplies of tin came to the Mediterranean world from the rich deposits in Cornwall, England, and some students of the problem have speculated that this was the source in earlier times as well, that Egypt and the other empires of the ancient Near East imported it all the way from there. Assyrian documents of the second millennium B.C. make it absolutely clear that there was an extensive caravan trade in tin going on in Mesopotamia, the Levant, and Asia Minor, with Mari, a commercial center on the upper Euphrates, serving as an *entrepôt*. Since there are no deposits in any of these places, the best guess has been that the tin came from further east, with Iran suggested as a possible source. But geologic reconnaissance has failed to find tin there. Recently, extensive deposits have been identified in western Afghanistan, and there is no reason why these could not have been the source; the tin would have been transported by caravan or boat or both to Mari and forwarded from there to various Near Eastern centers, including ports of the Levant whence it would have made its way by ship to Egypt.

Iron was not common in Egypt until long after the period that concerns us. Some few early objects of iron have been found, but analysis reveals that the metal was of meteoric origin. Among the treasures in Tutankhamen's tomb were an iron dagger and an iron headrest; they were included because of their rareness.

One other metal besides copper was widely used in Egypt—gold. Gold occurs in the veins of quartz-bearing rock all along the eastern desert. As early as the First Dynasty it was available in such quantity that in one tomb of the period there were pilasters adorned with strips of embossed sheet gold set no more than one centimeter apart and running from floor to ceiling. The richest deposits, however, were south of the border of Egypt proper, in Nubia and the Sudan. Some was placer mined along the riverbanks between the Second and Third cataracts, but most was mined from rock, especially in the region southeast of the Second Cataract. Thutmose III was able to bring out of the area no less than ten thousand ounces per year. In the reign of Amenhotep II there is a record of a shipment that needed as many as 150 porters. When the tomb of Tutankhamen was discovered, the world was astonished by the vast amount of gold in it; yet the treasures of this obscure pharaoh who died when very young must have been paltry compared with what went into the tomb of a mighty and aged potentate such as Thutmose III or Amenhotep III.

By the beginning of the third millennium B.C. Egypt's goldsmiths had mastered the working of the metal. They were able to cast it, hammer it, engrave and emboss it, solder it, draw it into wire. They beat it into sheets to cover the handles of weapons or to use on furniture or to be made, as in the case of Tutankhamen, into coffins and face masks. They fashioned it into jewelry, bracelets, and necklaces, often set with semiprecious stones such as turquoise, lapis lazuli, and amethyst.

Egypt's workers in stone run the gamut from humble masons to men who deserve to be called artists rather than craftsmen. We have already, in other connections, run across the workmen who, with monotonous but exacting labor, shaped and smoothed the stone that went into the pyramids and other great structures, as well as the practitioners of that fine minor art, the manufacture of stone vases. Now we turn to those at the top of the craft, the men who carved the myriad reliefs and statues that have given Egypt its place of honor in the history of art. Here again our astonishment is evoked by the magnificent quality of the work they were able to execute with the most rudimentary tools.

Like the makers of stone vases, they chose to work with some of the hardest rocks available, diorite, granite, basalt, schist. It was a major feat merely to quarry what they needed from the rock outcrops, such as monstrous chunks of quartzite for Amenhotep III's seventy-foot colossi or of granite for obelisks one hundred feet high. Pounding with dolerite balls or hammering with bronze—before the New Kingdom, with copper—or stone blunt-nosed picks, they would detach the top and sides of a block from the surrounding mass and then free the lower edge by cutting a series of slots along it and inserting wooden wedges, which were then wetted; the swelling of the wood would cause the piece to break free. Smaller pieces would be hauled on sleds to the riverside for transport to where they were needed. Larger pieces, such as those for colossal statues, would be first pounded into rough shape by dolerite balls and then transported; one relief shows a colossus being dragged by 172 men.

Soft stones like sandstone or some limestones could be worked with copper chisels, but no tool in the Egyptian mason's arsenal could possibly cut the likes of diorite or granite. The only way he was able to carve these and other hard rocks was by using his stone and copper tools along with an abrasive. He roughed out the shape by pounding with dolerite balls. Straight surfaces he could fashion by sawing, feeding an abrasive such as quartz sand into the slot to do the actual cutting. For fine work he first drilled wherever possible; the drills were tubular pieces of copper, rotated by hand or a bow, with the cutting edge turning in an abrasive. And the lustrous smooth surfaces he attained by patiently rubbing with a piece of stone over an abrasive.

Often the eyes were inlaid—and in this art Egyptian sculptors were matchless. For ordinary work they were content with inserting an eyeball of crystalline limestone with a piece of obsidian for the iris and pupil. In the best work there were eyelids of silver or copper, an eyeball of polished quartz, a cornea of rock crystal with a disk of brown resin for the iris, and, in a hole in the center of the iris, a plug of very dark brown or black resin for the pupil.

Still another group includes men who, no less than the sculptors, deserve the name of artist rather than craftsman—the painters of the scenes that decorate the walls of New Kingdom tombs and that tell in vivid detail so much about Egypt's daily life. The paintings have come through the ages in a remarkably good state of preservation. This is because the pigments for the most part were either mineral or derived from mineral substances. Egyptian artists made their white from chalk or gypsum, their black from soot, their gray from a mixture of the two. Yellow was from yellow ocher, red from red ocher or iron oxide, brown from brown ocher or iron oxide. Blue had to be made artificially, by heating malachite (copper ore) and sand and natron together, and green was either powdered malachite or blue mixed with yellow ocher. The paint was made by dissolving the pigments in a mixture of water and acacia gum or glue. Walls were covered with a coat of gypsum plaster, and the paint was applied when this had dried—in other words, a form of gouache and not fresco, which is applied while the plaster is wet. After the painting had dried, a protective coat of clear varnish was added, sometimes over the whole, sometimes over only certain colors such as the reds and yellows.

Sculptors, painters, cabinetmakers, jewelers, smiths—these were the country's most skilled workmen, the creators of the masterpieces that museums of the modern world are proud to display. We think of them as artists, but in the ancient Egyptian view they were just craftsmen, to be paid in rations like all other workmen. In common with all other Egyptian laborers, they belonged either to the pharaoh's household or one of his projects, to the household of some great official, or to a religious foundation. At Akhenaten's new city, his chief sculptor, the creator of the celebrated head of Nefertiti, was installed in a roomy house with his studio right off the entrance hall so that fashionable visitors had easy access to it. Nearby was a more modest house that included a studio for working in plaster, and this probably belonged to his chief assistant. Roundabout were still more modest habitations for the rank and file of his assistants. In the housing project for the workers employed on the royal tombs in Thebes, on the other hand, the houses were more or less alike; one identified as belonging to an architect was no bigger than any of the others.

The pay was in kind. There were monthly issues of food (bread, beans, beer, onions, dried meat, fat, salt, and so forth), issues of ointments at the end of the ten-day shifts the men worked, issues of clothing once a year; as Ramses II put it in an announcement he made to a group of quarrymen by way of assuring them of their pay, "each one of you will be cared for monthly. I have filled the storehouse for you with everything, with bread, meat, cakes for your food, sandals, linen, and much oil for anointing your heads every ten days and clothing you each year." Workers were classified according to what they did. At the top were foremen and scribes; then came draftsmen, sculptors, and painters; then quarrymen and masons; then, near the bottom of the list, unskilled labor, the hands who dug trenches or mixed and carried mortar; finally, at the very bottom, those who took care of the housing project's needs, who hauled the fuel and food and water or served as watchmen.

Men did not necessarily remain in the same bracket for life: craftsmen, like scribes, through work and ability could move up in the ranks. Among the necropolis workers at Thebes there was a certain Kha, who, starting at the level of draftsman, rose to the very top, achieving the title of architect—in his case a practicing architect, not just an administrator. He earned enough to decorate his eternal abode in far handsomer style than his earthly one and to fill it with treasures that included a fine ebony statue of himself and a gold cup bearing the name of one of his royal patrons, Amenhotep III.

On rare occasions an artist gained recognition over and above higher wages and promotion. A very few received the honor of mention in a patron's tomb; at Thebes, for example, a picture in a tomb shows the deceased seated at a banquet with his painter and his sculptor. Others got more tangible rewards, gifts of landed property or funeral endowments.

In good times working conditions were not at all bad. The men did a ten-day shift, after which they got a certain amount of time off. And the authorities seem to have been lenient about absence; it was allowed not only for sickness but for nursing the sick. Sickness itself was liberally interpreted. One man was excused from work because—or so he alleged—he had been beaten up by his wife.

But when times were bad the men suffered: their wages were not paid, and this meant that they simply went hungry. A peasant on a farm could always scrounge something to put in his belly, at the very least go down to the bank and cut some papyrus stalks to chew, but Egypt's laborers, closed off in their housing projects, depended totally on their wages. Toward the very end of the period we are concerned with, about 1160 B.C., at the necropolis in Thebes things got to the point where the men refused to work—the first strike in history that we know of. A precious papyrus document that somehow survived provides the details. By the middle of November the men's rations were two months in arrears; two paydays, the first of October and the first of November, had passed without their receiving a thing. So they left the precincts of the housing project shouting "We are hungry!" and sat down en masse back of a temple at the edge of the bordering farmland. The supervisors pleaded with them to go back to work, even swore, "You may come (back), for we have the word of Pharaoh!" but the men were adamant and returned to their houses only when night fell.

They walked out again the following day, and the day after that they even invaded the Ramesseum, the august complex around the grave of the great Ramses II. Immediately there was a scurrying of high officialdom, by then sufficiently upset to listen to what the men had to say: "We have reached this place because of hunger, because of thirst, without clothing, without ointments, without fish, without vegetables! Write to Pharaoh, our good lord, about it, and write to the Vizier, our superior. Act so that we may live!" This finally worked, and the men collected their October rations. But they had their minds made up—they wanted their pay for the current month as well, so they marched upon police headquarters, where the chief of police promised to help: "Look, I give you my answer: Go up (to your homes) and gather your gear and lock your doors and take your wives and your children. And I will go ahead of you to the Temple (of Thutmose III) and will let you sit there tomorrow." The men had to put in eight days of sitting before they got paid.

Two weeks later the first of the next month came around, again no pay, so again they walked out. This time their statements contained accusations of fraud. The vizier himself was drawn into the dispute. Through a spokesman, he issued an announcement to the effect that "if it should happen that there is nothing in the granary itself, I shall give you what I may find!" that is, attend to the matter personally. Whatever the reason, whether he could find nothing or preferred to forget his promise, the gangs went back to their sit-downs beside temples in the vicinity. Once the mayor of Thebes took pity on them and issued fifty sacks of grain to tide them over—and was promptly accused of malfeasance, of taking improperly from another source; "This is a great crime which he is doing!" was the cry. Our records cease at this point, so we have no idea how the problem was finally settled—if it ever was.

However badly off the necropolis workers at Thebes may have been at times, their life was a paradise compared with that of the wretches assigned to work in the mines. Mining was the worst blot on the social escutcheon of every ancient state, whether the Egypt of the pharaohs, the Athens of Pericles, the Rome of the emperors. We have a report, drawn up by a Greek geographer of the second century B.C., on the ·

mining of gold in the Sudan desert. He is describing the system used by the Ptolemies, rulers of Egypt at that time, who manned the mines with prisoners of war, convicts, and the like, but things could hardly have been much better under the pharaohs:

The worst of fates falls to the lot of those whom the tyrannical government sends off to the bitter slavery of the gold mines, some to suffer along with their wives and children, some without. . . . The rock of the mountains in which the gold is found is sheer and very hard. They burn wood fires and render it spongy with heat, and then go at working it, cutting the parts softened up with quarrying tools. . . .

Those who are young and strong quarry the gleaming stone with iron picks, delivering their blows not with any particular skill but just force. They cut numerous galleries in the rock, never straight but as the ore-bearing part directs, sometimes upward, sometimes downward, sometimes in a bend to the left, sometimes crooked and contorted like tree roots. They do their quarrying with lamps bound to their foreheads, following the white gleam like a vein. Constantly shifting the position of their bodies, they knock down chunks—not according to their bodily condition and strength but to the foreman's eye, who never fails to administer punishment with the whip.

Young boys, creeping through the galleries hacked out by the miners, laboriously collect what has fallen down on the gallery floor and carry it outside the entrance. From them the rock is taken over by the more elderly and many of the feeble, who bring it to the so-called choppers. For the men who are still under thirty and have the appearance of being strong are given stone mortars, and they pound the rock vigorously with iron pestles until they have made the biggest piece the size of a pea. Then they measure out to others the rock pounded to this size.

Now starts the work of the women who were arrested and put in custody along with their husbands or parents. A large number of grinding mills are placed in a row, and the pounded rock is put in them. The women take their places, three to a turning bar, and grind away. They are a sad sight, their clothes girded up and just enough to cover their private parts. They grind until they have reduced what was measured out to them to the consistency of fine flour.

All who suffer the fate just described feel that death is more desirable than life.

CHAPTER IX

Religion

"[The Egyptians] consider all animals, both wild and tame, to be sacred. . . . The various breeds have keepers appointed, in some cases men and in others women, who are responsible for feeding them; the office of keeper is hereditary, being handed down from father to son. . . . Anyone who deliberately kills an animal is punished with death, while the penalty for an accidental killing is whatever the priests choose to impose. For killing an ibis or hawk, whether deliberate or not, death is mandatory. . . . Cats that have died are taken to Bubastis and there embalmed and buried in sacred receptacles; and dogs are buried in sacred tombs in the towns they belong to. . . . Field-mice and hawks are taken to Buto, ibises to Hermopolis. . . . Some Egyptians worship the crocodile as sacred, others not, and treat them as enemies. The center for the belief in crocodiles is Thebes and around Lake Moeris [in the Faiyum]. Here the locals tame and keep one crocodile, putting rings of glass or gold in its ears and bracelets on its front feet. They give special food and offerings to it, treating it in the finest way possible as long as it lives. When it dies they embalm it and bury it in a sacred tomb." Herodotus noted all this about the middle of the fifth century B.C., when Egypt had lost its vitality and degenerated into a fossilized, ghost-ridden society, a museum of outworn ways and beliefs. What he was observing was the dimly understood superstitious cultivation of forms of animal worship that went back to Egypt's earliest days and, like so many aspects of her life, lived on, undergoing adaptation and change but never dying out.

Indeed, objects of worship would be the last candidates for extinction, for religion permeated an Egyptian's total existence. In his eyes, every detail of his own life and of the life about him, whether the annual inundation of the Nile that spelled hunger or plenty for the whole nation or the chance death of his cat, was a specific, calculated act of god. We of the West can place religion in a compartment all its own, we can say, "Render unto Caesar the things that are Caesar's and to God the things that are God's," but not an Egyptian. His Caesar was the pharaoh, and the pharaoh was a god. Egypt's glorious artistic creations were inspired by religion and religion alone. The Egyptian artist's forte was sculpture, because in Egyptian thinking a statue erected in tomb or temple was a way of ensuring an individual's existence for eternity after death, and all who could afford it provided themselves with at least one. Egyptians never ordered their sculptors to carve portrait statues or busts to display in a public square or in a niche at home; that was a concept for other civilizations to develop. Similarly, the monuments of Egyptian architecture are all religious—pyramids and other types of tombs, temple chapels and halls and sanctums. These were the only structures made of stone, since they were to last forever. The dwellings the Egyptians put up for their life on earth, not excepting the palaces of their kings, were of mud brick and have all but disappeared.

Even in politics the ubiquitous presence of religion is clear. The great administrative officials at the pharaoh's court were at the same time prelates of the church: Hatshepsut's factotum Senmut, for example, included among his multitudinous titles Sole Companion and Steward of Amon, Prophet of Amon, and others like it. When a pharaoh put men to work for thirty years on a pyramid or called up a veritable army to hack out a three-hundred-ton chunk of granite for an obelisk and transport it from the quarries at Aswan hundreds of miles to a temple precinct and erect it there, he was not whipping an oppressed people into doing repugnant tasks, but simply canalizing a willing service on behalf of the gods.

Prehistoric Egyptians, like most primitive peoples, were sensitive to natural phenomena, above all the behavior of the animals they came in contact with. They early observed the tender care of a cow for her young, the strength of a crocodile, the ferocity of a lion; they were so impressed that they came to worship the beasts for their special powers, with villages or communities or tribes having their particular favorites. As a consequence, very early in Egyptian history, long before the country became a political whole, its various towns each acquired an animal deity. Bubastis and Buto in the delta became, respectively, the home of the cult of the cat goddess Bast and the cobra goddess Edjo, Hermopolis and Lycopolis in middle Egypt of the ibis god Thoth and the jackal god Wepwawet, Elephantine in Upper Egypt of the ram god Khnum, and so on. With their ingrained habit of never abandoning the old, the Egyptians continued to worship these queer divinities long after they had adopted anthropomorphic gods and had developed a fairly sophisticated theology. Right down to the time when Herodotus made his visit, and for many centuries thereafter, a crocodile incarnating the spirit of the crocodile god Sobek lolled at Crocodilopolis, the cat of Bast at Bubastis, and so on.

Worship of animals and nature commonly occurs in very early societies, which are dominated by the world roundabout and exist at its mercy. In most a moment arrives when they learn to come to grips with nature, to master it; this awakens a sense of man's importance, and deities begin to assume the form of man as well as the forms of animals or plants. So it was with the Egyptians: sometime before the rise of the First Dynasty, anthropomorphism makes its appearance. In their traditional way, they introduced it gradually and blended it with what they already had.

One of the first deities to show the effects of the new fusion was Hathor, goddess of love and childbirth: she was given a human body and head but retained an element from her ancient animal manifestation, a pair of cow's horns. Other kept their animal heads and acquired human bodies. Thus Thoth, the scribes' patron deity, became an ibis-headed man. Anubis, who was guardian of tombs and in time was promoted to a role as judge in the underworld as well, became a jackal-headed man. Khnum, originally a ram, and since the Egyptians considered the animal particularly prolific, associated with creation, turned into a ram-headed man often portrayed as a divine potter modeling men on a potter's wheel. Gods that arose later were anthropomorphic from the very beginning. Ptah, the god of craftsmen, who first appears in history when Memphis was founded as capital of the Old Kingdom, was always portrayed as human, and Amon, the obscure Theban god who, emerging during the Twelfth Dynasty, rose to become supreme head of the Egyptian pantheon, was usually so.

The early anthropomorphic deities such as Ptah figure in the creation story, of which the Egyptians had several versions. Most of these rather literally pictured life as coming into being much the way Egypt's land re-emerged after the annual inundation of the Nile. In the beginning there was a dark, watery void. There came a time when this void subsided to permit the emergence of the first primordial hillock of earth—just as the subsiding of the Nile flood permits hillocks of mud to appear with their promise of the life-giving harvest that will follow. On the hillock was the creator-god Atum, who, in some way, brought living things into the world. In the version of the story that arose at Memphis, Ptah, the god of the place, was held to have brought creation about by his "heart and tongue"—that is to say, by mind and speech, by conceiving of the idea of a universe and executing his conception with a verbal command; the physical happenings may have taken place as described in the myth of the void, the hillock, and Atum, but those physical happenings were the result of Ptah's thought and order. Ptah, despite the significant role he is here given and his undoubted importance otherwise, tended to remain the local deity of Memphis and never forged ahead to become of national importance.

One god who most certainly did was Re, god of the sun, an understandable promotion for a deity in a land that basked in its benign rays.

Re's ascent dates from the Fifth Dynasty, whose pharaohs did not try to outdo their predecessors' pyramid tombs, those structures that dramatically proclaimed the deceased's mighty place in the scheme of things, but, calling themselves sons of Re, built ever more magnificent temples for their father's worship. These were erected at Heliopolis, now a suburb of Cairo, the traditional site of the cult. The version of the creation story current here held that the primordial hillock was located at Heliopolis. A hill in the area was identified with the momentous spot, and on it stood a primitive stone, looking rather like a squat obelisk; it became the inspiration for the slender soaring shafts set up by later dynasties. Re's temples all had open courts where the service could appropriately be carried out in the full rays of the sun, and where there stood a replica of the holy stone of the primordial hillock.

The chief anthropomorphic god was Amon, who, under the title of Amon Re, associated the power of the great sun deity with his own. Amon was the unseen god—the name means "hidden"—who is immanent in all things. He first appears as a local Theban deity during the Twelfth Dynasty, whose kings came from Thebes and elevated the place into the nation's capital. His rise to prominence began in the Eighteenth, when he was worshiped as the god who had given victory over the Hyksos to its pharaohs, enabling them finally to rid the homeland of the hated foreign invader. As Egypt acquired an empire, his power grew to embrace the widespread territories over which it held sway. A shrine was established for him at Karnak, not far from the royal palace, and it became fabulously rich on the god's share of the profits of empire. As time passed, it turned into one of the most massive temple precincts ever built, spreading over acres and acquiring new structures for more than a thousand years. By the time the empire came to a close, Amon's priests owned the lion's share of Egypt's wealth and rivaled the pharaoh in power.

The pharaoh was a god who was not merely anthropomorphic but a veritable man. He represented the Egyptians in the councils of the gods. He ruled—he could not help but rule—in accordance with *maat,* the eternal and unchanging order, the true and proper and just order, that is built into the universe. His death was his way of leaving to join his fellow gods. His son who replaced him was the same god, and so it had been from the beginning of time and would be to its end. The Egyptians, however, with all their conservative and static ways were not immune to what was happening about them, and in the course of time the pharaoh's status inevitably was modified. His high point was the Fourth Dynasty, when he was able to command the materials and manpower to build a great pyramid as his tomb. By the very next dynasty, as we have noted, he had yielded place to the sun god and by the Eighteenth Dynasty to Amon.

When a pharaoh died he both joined up with the sun god in his circuit of the heavens and at the same time became Osiris, king of the dead in the underworld. The son who took over the throne became Horus, the dutiful child of Osiris who had avenged his father's death (how a god could die, or a post-mortem pharaoh be both in heaven and below the earth, is troubling only to our way of thinking, not an Egyptian's). This brings us to the only members of the pantheon who came to exercise an influence outside of Egypt, the trinity of Osiris, Isis, and Horus.

According to the story, Osiris was murdered by his jealous brother Seth, who savagely cut the corpse up into pieces and scattered them. Isis, Osiris' wife, with admirable conjugal devotion, patiently collected the pieces and by her magic put them together and resuscitated her husband. Horus, their son, with equally admirable filial devotion, hounded Seth, forced him into a fight, and defeated him, thereby avenging his father. The resurrected Osiris (the resurrection element in the story may point to his having been at some time a god of vegetation, one of those primitive deities who consistently figure in resurrection myths) became god of the underworld, identified with the dead pharaoh. Horus, the son, became identified with the living pharaoh, a process helped along by the fact that ever since the First Dynasty, the pharaoh had been identified with a falcon god also called Horus.

In the days of the New Kingdom the trinity gained increasingly in importance. The dead came before Osiris in the underworld for their last judgment. In the upper world Isis, thanks to the magic that had enabled her to bring her husband back to life, became a healing goddess, and, thanks to her devotion to husband and son, the mother goddess par excellence. From the seventh century B.C. on she was Egypt's most widely worshiped deity, and when Rome had converted Egypt into a province of its vast empire, her cult spread from the Valley of the Nile to the farthest reaches of the Roman world. There it left its imprint upon Christianity; representations of Isis and Horus are pagan versions of the Madonna and child.

Despite the many all-powerful national deities, Egypt's local gods never lost their importance. They were usually conceived of as being immanent in their place of origin; so in each locale temples arose to house the resident divinity. In the desert near Memphis was the home of Sekhmet, a fierce goddess with lion's head atop a woman's body who caused and cured plague. At Hermopolis, midway between Memphis and Thebes, was the center of worship for Thoth. At Dendera, near Thebes, was Hathor's temple. Some minor deities, favorites among workmen and peasants, were ubiquitous, like Bes, the lion-headed dwarf who scared off evil spirits, or Thoueris, the hippopotamus god, who ensured fertility and safe childbirth.

With their catholic taste for deities, the Egyptians cheerfully accepted foreign immigrants. Government and military personnel stationed abroad easily fell into the habit of worshiping the gods of the locale, often equating them with their nearest Egyptian equivalent. In New Kingdom times, when thousands of prisoners of war, mercenaries, traders, and other non-Egyptians came to settle in the Valley of the Nile bringing their gods with them, these triumphantly survived transplanting, particularly the Semitic deities. Shamash, the sun god, was identified with Re, the goddess Baalath with Hathor, the god Baal with Seth. From the late Eighteenth Dynasty on we find priests of Baal and Astarte, the notorious Semitic goddess of love, in Egypt, and Egyptian children begin to bear names like Astartemheb, "Astarte is in Festival."

Within this welter of major and minor deities there yet can be distinguished some main lines of Egyptian religious thought. The most obvious is the belief in a life after death, a key tenet that deserves a chapter of its own. Another is a vague, ill-defined belief in one single supreme god; this found its most distinct expression during the reign of the heretical Pharaoh Akhenaten, to whom we will shortly turn. Yet another is that, at the creation of the world, a divine order was established, one that embodied *maat*, a key word which, as John Wilson, one of our most thoughtful Egyptologists, explains, had some of the same flexibility as our English terms *right, just, true,* and *in order.* It was

the cosmic form of harmony, order, stability, and security, coming down from the first creation as the organizing quality of created phenomena and reaffirmed at the accession of each god-king of Egypt. . . . So the relationship of beings was not something which had to be worked out painfully in an evolution toward even better conditions but was magnificently free from change, experiment, or evolution, since it had been fully good from the Beginning and needed only to be reaffirmed in its unchanging rightness.

Aspects of *maat,* even of the divine kingship, could be subject to misfortune or challenge, but these were only temporary; the nature of the world was that it would ever return to its original rightness, as a sponge reassumes its original shape. This was a concept that arose from, and was fostered by, the land's geography and climate, the barriers of desert that gave it security, the sunny days and life-giving river that made existence so much easier than elsewhere. The Egyptians held by this belief for centuries, until the heartache and the thousand natural shocks that flesh is heir to disabused even their ingrained optimism. We know the Egyptians by the physical remains they have left behind, which reflect overwhelmingly their concern with death, and by the writings of Greeks and Romans, who saw them after they had degenerated into a static superstition-ridden society. Thus our first impression is of a timid, fear-haunted people cowering before terrifying powers, an impression that could not be more wrong. In the great days of the pharaohs, the Egyptian, confident that his world was divinely good, that his ruler represented him amid the very councils of the gods, was garrulous, cheerful, optimistic, often so sure of himself and his future that he turned cocky and arrogant.

An Egyptian temple was not designed, like our places of worship, for accommodating congregations. Though it was usually large and often grandiose, its *raison d'être* was to house a rather small cult image of a god. This was invariably tucked away in an inner sanctum, hidden from all eyes save those of the very few qualified to look upon it. From the exterior, a temple's most prominent features were an enceinte wall and a massive gateway, or pylon as it is called, which, towering over the rest, formed the façade. Thus it was just the opposite of a Greek temple: it turned inward, it was to be seen and enjoyed from the inside.

The architects of the Old Kingdom built with limestone, which, though handsome, had a shortcoming: an architrave made out of it would not span more than three yards without giving way, and this severely limited the amount of free space that could be enclosed. The architects of the great temples of the New Kingdom turned to sandstone, which is softer than limestone, shows the effects of weathering much more readily, and is not nearly so handsome; but sandstone architraves will span eight yards or more. The temples of New Kingdom times and later at Karnak, Luxor, Dendera, Edfu, and many other sites are of this prosaic but useful stone.

These temples all display the same basic elements. People entered by way of a gate in the pylon to pass into an open court with colonnades on either side; beyond that was a lofty covered hall with its ceiling borne on columns, and, finally, the private sanctuary of the god, concealed behind walls and surrounded by small service chambers. The bastionlike pylon discouraged intruders, and the public, when witnessing or taking part in certain portions of the ceremonies, was allowed only into the court. The temple proper, vast though it might be, formed only a part of a greater complex. This included living quarters for the permanent staff, workshops, schools, a sacred pool, granaries and other kinds of storage—in short, all the facilities needed to support the large and miscellaneous community that served the god.

The biggest and best known of the New Kingdom temples is the one built in honor of Amon at Karnak, on the east bank of the Nile just north of Thebes. It grew out of a modest shrine that was erected in the Twelfth Dynasty for the god when he was but a minor local divinity. From the Eighteenth Dynasty on, as the empire expanded and the national gratitude toward Amon with it, the pharaohs contributed additions until the temple structures eventually covered an area of four hundred by five hundred yards. Around the original Twelfth Dynasty structure Thutmose I made significant additions including a pair of pylons; Hatshepsut set up two soaring obelisks outside the pylon; and Thutmose III added yet another pylon and more covered halls, closing in the lower part of his despised stepmother's obelisks (they stuck up through holes in the roof). The most imposing part of all was the work of Seti I and his son Ramses II, the vast Hypostyle Hall that covers 5,800 square yards and gets its name from the forest of 134 gigantic columns, 69 feet high and 33 feet in circumference, that hold up the ceiling; each is carved with scenes depicting the king worshiping Amon.

About two miles south of Karnak, near the modern town of Luxor, or Opet, to give it its ancient name, stands a second great temple to Amon. Despite an outer court and pylon that were built later than the main structure and not properly aligned with it, the temple is more harmonious and coherent in design than Karnak, largely because only one man, Amenhotep III, was responsible for it and it reflects his taste. There were two obelisks in front of the pylon, of which only one is left; the other now adorns the Place de la Concorde in Paris.

The most insatiable builder of all the pharaohs was Ramses II. His forte was grandioseness—particularly when it came to statues of himself. In the first court of the Ramesseum, his mortuary temple, he erected one of Aswan granite that is fifty-six feet tall and weighs about a thousand tons; the head measures more than six feet from ear to ear. And even it is smaller than the four, all sixty-five feet high, that dominate the façade of his temple at Abu Simbel on the Nile between the First and Second Cataracts (it now stands high on the hillside, having been moved in the 1960s to avoid being inundated by the waters backing up behind the Aswan High Dam). Ramses had a highhanded habit of cannibalizing stone for his projects from the structures of his predecessors, or even expropriating their works by crossing out their names and substituting his own.

In an Egyptian temple the service went on ceaselessly from dawn to dusk to ensure that the spirit of the god be content to dwell in the cult image hidden away in the interior and not abandon it. At dawn the officiating priest approached the tabernacle that contained the awesome statue. It had been closed and sealed as part of the evening ceremonies of the day before; he broke the clay seals and, amid incantations and prescribed prayers and clouds of incense, drew forth the sacred image—probably of wood lavishly adorned with gold—and then did for it what the palace valets did for the pharaoh: he bathed and perfumed it, dressed it in clothes and jewelry, garlanded it with fresh flowers, and, replacing it in its shrine, offered it food and drink. All day long the ceremony went on, a continuum of music, dance, and hymns. At dusk the priest shut the door, resealed it, and backed out of the room, simultaneously sweeping away with a broom the traces of his footprints.

Amon was an anthropomorphic god, so his spirit was able to be conceived of as inhabiting a cult image. In the many instances of gods incarnated in an animal figure, the ritual necessarily was considerably different. At Crocodilopolis, the cult site of Sobek, the crocodile god, the service took place around the pool where the sacred animal lived, and the highlight was the ritual feeding of the creature. Presumably the same was true at Hermopolis, where Thoth's ibis was kept, at Bubastis, where Bast's cat lived, and so on.

In the most ancient times, it must have been the pharaoh himself who carried out the god's toilette, but other demands on his time soon made him turn the task over to high priests acting on his behalf. As they went through the ritual they were aided by lesser clergy known as the pure or the purifiers, who were entrusted with the censing, dressing, carrying of ritual utensils, and other chores, and who helped to hand the image in and out of the tabernacle. The ranks of the lesser clergy included as well guardians and readers of the sacred books, experts in ritual procedure, and horologers, who watched the heavens in order to set the hours of the daily rites and the calendar dates of festivals. Only the few priests authorized to enter the innermost sanctum and officiate at the ceremony were full-time clergymen. The minor orders were made up of civilians who forsook their secular life one month out of every four to live in the temple and serve the god. This was true of the various specialists as well, the scribes, singers, musicians, even overseers of the temple artisans.

Priests and specialists were divided into four rotating shifts, each having, as just mentioned, one month on duty and three off. The "pure" maintained a rigid ritual cleanliness during their month. They all were circumcised, for in their case this was not optional. In addition they shaved their heads, bathed frequently and at fixed times, dressed only in pure white linen (even leather was taboo; they had to wear sandals of papyrus), and forswore relations with women. When back in civilian life, they could do and wear what they liked, but the tendency arose to distinguish themselves with a modified clerical garb, shaven head, and instead of a full-length gown, a long kilt that left the torso bare.

The temples, as we noted before, had schools attached to them, and it is very likely that boys intending to enter the clergy started by going through the regular course for scribes. There were no seminary classes, so the embryo priests, like all the other graduates, received on-the-job training. Some of their number, if not all, put in some time in the scriptorium, a place where sacred books were transcribed or new ones compiled from ancient sources.

A major temple was headed by a body of prelates. There were four in the body that ran Amon's at Karnak, of whom the so-called First Prophet was the high priest, responsible not only for the vast complex immediately under him but for others as well, since Amon during New Kingdom times was the acknowledged king of all the gods. The high priest of Amon and the high priests of Ptah at Memphis and of Re at Heliopolis, since they officiated as the pharaoh's representatives, were personally appointed by him and invested by him in a special ceremony.

Perhaps he chose their fellow members in the governing bodies, but the clergy of the ranks below were selected either by the vizier or the high priests themselves. Since there was no sharp division in Egypt between church and state, the high priesthood often was just another hat worn by some great civil official: Ptahmose, one of Amenhotep III's viziers, was high priest at Karnak, while Amenhotep-son-of-Hapu, Amen-hotep III's official-of-all-work, somehow had enough free time from his recruiting for the army and his setting up of colossal statues to serve as First Prophet in a temple in his home town in the delta. Though there was some movement up in the priestly ranks, there was the same tendency there that we have noted elsewhere to keep good things within the family: clerics trained their sons, nephews, or sons-in-law to take over from them.

Amon had priestesses as well as priests serving him. They played no part in the daily sacred toilette—that was for men only—but served as temple musicians and singers. One group, headed by the queen or one of the princesses, was known as the Concubines of the God—since Amon bathed, dressed, and ate like a pharaoh, it followed that he had to have a harem. The ranks of the priestesses included wives and daughters of courtiers as well as more humble women.

During the day, while the ritual was going on in the inner sanctum, people would wander into the outer court or other areas where statues of the deity happened to be on view and lay before them votive offer-ings, frequently a little piece of stone with an engraving of the god on it, sometimes with a single ear, more often with a number of ears; one example has no fewer than 378. Presumably the god who received these multieared figures got the hint. Some temple precincts housed steles that had the magic power of healing—steles of Horus, for example, carrying an inscription that told the story of how, when bitten by a snake, he had been cured by Thoth. The very humble, who would be apt to feel overawed amid the splendors of Amon's temple at Karnak or similar places, preferred to patronize more modest facilities. The work-men at Thebes' necropolis favored a local snake goddess who had a shrine on a hill overlooking their housing project. They also maintained at least four shrines dedicated to Amenhotep I; since he had been the first pharaoh to have a tomb at Thebes, he was the founding father, as it were, of their community.

The daily ritual in the temples, the casual visits of suppliants to beg a favor or leave a thank offering, was punctuated by festivals. Every god, whether local or national, had at least one annually, an occasion when he left the secrecy of his tabernacle and displayed himself to his worshipers. Many fell, as festivals have always fallen in agricultural lands, at the moments in the year that were critical for the farmer, before the sowing or after the harvest. In Egypt, where such moments were controlled by the behavior of the Nile, the festivals tended to fall during the season of the Inundation, June to September, when the fields were under water and the peasants, spared their endless round of sowing, dike making and repairing, irrigating, and the like, had some moments of leisure. New Year's Day, for example, which naturally called for a celebration, came in July, the month in which the inundation was gathering force, and one could thank the gods if it looked abundant or invoke their help if meager.

In Egypt, where religion outstripped all other interests and where a convenient river made traveling anywhere in the country relatively easy, festivals, even for local deities, could count on a good turnout. As Herodotus reports:

The Egyptians celebrate festivals not once but several times a year. The one they are most enthusiastic about takes place at Bubastis . . . that at Busiris ranks second . . . at Sais third, at Heliopolis fourth . . . at Buto fifth . . . at Papremis sixth. When they gather at Bubastis this is what happens. They go there on the river, men and women together, a big crowd of each in each boat. As they sail, some of the women keep clicking castanets and some of the men playing on the pipes, and the rest, both men and women, sing and beat time with their hands. Whenever they pass a town they bring their craft close inshore and do as follows: some of the women keep on as I have just described, but others scream and make fun of the women in the town, still others dance, and still others stand up and expose themselves. They carry on this way at every town along the river. And when they arrive at Bubastis, they celebrate the occasion with great sacrifices, and more wine is consumed at this one festival than during the whole rest of the year. According to the locals, up to seven hundred thousand people gather there, including men and women but not children.

Seven hundred thousand people, more wine consumed than during the rest of the year—there is no doubt a good deal of exaggeration here; the information, after all, came to Herodotus not from official records but from bystanders he happened to chat with. Nevertheless, it *was* a great occasion, and we are left in no doubt about how important such festivals were in Egyptian life: they were the moments when the peasant and workman were able to relax totally, when they could for once eat and drink their fill because their god was paying for it.

Of all the festivals none could match for size and grandeur the Beautiful Feast of Opet. This was the occasion when Amon left his temple at Karnak to make an annual trip to his other temple in Thebes at Opet (Luxor), the one and only time during the year when he generously displayed himself to his worshipful public. Moreover, it was the longest of the festivals; during the time of Thutmose III it went on for ten days, by the time of Ramses II it had lengthened to twenty-four, still later to twenty-seven. It fell during the second and third months of the Inundation, precisely the time when most of the populace was free to enjoy it.

The ceremony began with a monumental procession. We have a good idea of what it was like from scenes painted on temple walls at Luxor and elsewhere. A throng of priests left the grounds at Karnak, some of them carrying on their shoulders three portable boats, and the others purifying the way with censers or shading it with giant fans of ostrich feathers. In one boat, marked by a ram's head at bow and stern, was the precious image of Amon; in another, marked by women's heads, his consort Mut; in the third, marked by falcon heads, his son Khonsu. Headed by a musician banging on a tambourine, the procession made its way to the riverside, where three sumptuous barges, each some sixty to seventy yards long and fitted with a canopied dais, were waiting to receive the distinguished passengers. Each shrine with its cult image was placed on a dais, statues and sphinxes brought from the temple were placed all about it, and in front of it, just as in a temple, were set a pair of miniature obelisks sheathed in gold. The barges were made of the finest Lebanon cedar and decorated lavishly with gold and gems. Since they were too heavy to proceed under their own power, an army of men on the riverside hauled them with tow ropes, urged on not only by their commanders but by the mob that had gathered there to catch a glimpse of the god and to partake in the excitement. Once the tugging men got the barges in the clear, these were taken under tow by boats and, with a fleet of miscellaneous smaller craft all about them, were pulled up the river. A mob of spectators lined both banks; here and there were tents and stalls where drinks were served, where carcasses were cut up and cooked and served, where foods of all kinds were available. Military bands pounded the drums, dancing girls whirled and twisted. At Luxor a procession emerged from the temple leading oxen with gilded horns for the god's table. The barges were moored, the shrines removed, and with the pharaoh himself leading the parade, the gods were carried into the temple, where they resumed their accustomed secrecy. In the meantime, however, the drinking and eating and dancing and singing went on ceaselessly and continued to go on for the duration of Amon's stay. On the last day the events of the first were re-enacted, only in reverse, and perhaps more soberly.

During his great festival, Amon entertained with open hand. Preserved records show that during one particular year the minimum daily requirement was 11,341 loaves of bread and 385 jugs of beer, the loaves of extra size and the beer of extra strength; the anniversary of a king's coronation, no mean occasion, required less than half that.

Amon left the darkness of his sanctuary for yet another annual trip, though a much shorter one of only ten days, the Feast of the Valley. It was in response to the pharaoh's invitation to the god to visit the temples of the dead. The pharaoh put him aboard the sacred barge and took him across the river, where the royal ancestors lay buried in the rock-cut tombs of the Valley of the Kings. During his stay Amon was understood to receive visits from the gods of the dead. The living profited by the occasion to visit the tombs and bring the deceased food, drink, and fresh flowers.

Despite the general carnival atmosphere, there were moments during these festivals that could be deadly serious. During his public appearances, the god might be asked vital questions—to decide a bitter law suit, to indicate his choice of candidate for a high office, even to settle quarrels about the succession to the throne. Once during Hatshepsut's reign, those backing her rival, the young Thutmose, took advantage of the god's public appearance at a festival to ask for a sign as to who should be pharaoh. The god could make a forward inclination for assent, backward for dissent, point to a candidate, and the like. How it was done is anybody's guess. Presumably the priests in charge not only worked out the mechanics but consulted beforehand with the appropriate authorities as to what the divine decision should be.

At the other end of the scale from Amon's festivals were the local celebrations run by humble groups. The necropolis workers of Thebes, for example, held one in honor of their founding father, Pharaoh Amenhotep I, in which they ate, drank, sang, and danced for four days. And all who carried on the ritual actions—shaded the god or fanned him or censed him—were workmen.

There were still other occasions for festivals besides those for the gods. The pharaoh's accession, coronation, and military victories all called for celebrating. Then there were his jubilees, the *sed* festivals, which were supposed to renew the royal vitality and reaffirm his right to rule Upper and Lower Egypt. Not only notables but gods gathered for the occasion from all over the land, arriving in splendid sacred barges. The first *sed* came only on completion of thirty years on the throne, but after that a pharaoh could hurry them up; presumably he needed more frequent refreshing. Amenhotep III, for example, had a second in the thirty-fourth year and a third in the thirty-seventh.

All the festivals we have described, whether public or private, whether annual or occasional, whether for king or god, were done in the typical Egyptian spirit. There was no fasting or solemn prayer, no penances—just music, song, dance, feasting, and lots of drinking.

CHAPTER X

A Maverick Pharaoh

About 1390 B.C. Amenhotep III ascended the throne. He carried on his predecessors' vigorous way of life only to the extent of going after big game (he boasts of bagging a grand total of 102 lions), leaving the leading and exercising of the troops to others. After some ten years, he gave up even this much bodily activity: in his inscriptions he refers to himself as a "lord of strength" and a "fierce-eyed lion"; it was the strength and ferocity of a menagerie lion. His ancestors had gained and maintained Egypt's empire by the force of her arms; Amenhotep maintained it by her gold and prestige. He made alliances with the neighboring rulers in Syria, the Levant, Mesopotamia, and Asia Minor and cemented them by means of gifts and marriages, adding their sisters and daughters to his harem; he was negotiating for yet another Asiatic bride shortly before he died, an old and ailing man whose reign had lasted thirty-eight years.

The one activity he did indulge in was building, particularly in honor of Amon and himself. He put up the fine temple at Luxor, where Amon made his annual visit during the Beautiful Feast of Opet. Across the river he built a mortuary chapel for himself that was the biggest in history (the two great fifty-foot-high statues that we have mentioned earlier stood in front of it). In the vicinity he erected a sprawling new palace that covered eighty acres. Deep in the Sudan below the Third Cataract he built a temple for himself and Amon and not far away another for Tiy, his queen; despite her nonroyal birth and despite the Asiatic ladies of lofty pedigree in his harem, he was devoted to his Great Wife, associated her with the important affairs of state, and lavished gifts on her, even going as far as to dig her a private lake. During the last years of his life he may have adopted his eldest son, Amenhotep IV, as coregent; perhaps he wanted to shuck off all cares of state and devote himself full time to his building and his harem. As it happened, the son's coronation, whether as coregent or as pharaoh in his own right at the old man's death, opened a unique and most strange period in Egyptian history.

At the outset all seemed normal enough. He took a wife, Nefertiti, and she promptly bore him the first of six daughters. He had himself portrayed in the time-honored fashion of the pharaohs, with trim athletic figure in a regal pose. Within a short time, however, it became patently clear that the new king had ideas very much his own. He began to evince a marked disinterest in Amon, the dynasty's pampered patron deity, and a marked interest in the Aten, the sun disk. In doing so he was on well-trodden ground, venturing into nothing unorthodox. Re, god of the sun, was, as we have seen, one of the oldest and most respected Egyptian deities; the Aten was simply his visible aspect, and three generations of pharaohs had already turned it into an object of worship of high standing. Amenhotep III, for all his manifest predilection for Amon, had named his flagship the *Splendor of Aten*.

But his son's devotion, it quickly transpired, was of a different order. Not very long after gaining the throne in 1353, he put up a temple for the Aten just east of Amon's vast complex at Karnak, and in its court he included a series of colossal statues of himself that must have hit contemporaries like a thunderbolt, so violent was their break with the past. Such statues of previous pharaohs had always represented them either in jubilee costume or in mummy wrappings as resurrected immortals, assimilated to Osiris, king of the underworld. Amenhotep IV chose to represent himself as a living king in the costume of the living and to add attributes pointing to a relation with sun worship.

Even more iconoclastic, instead of representing himself in the traditional heroic fashion, he had his sculptors give him an elongated jaw, scrawny neck, drooping shoulders, potbelly, spindly shanks, and buttocks as thick and rounded as a woman's. As if to underline this feminine aspect, in the statues of him nude, he had them show him without genitalia. The portrayals were so outré that the nineteenth-century archaeologists who discovered them were convinced they were dealing with representations of a woman, some queen. When the deciphering of the inscriptions revealed beyond any doubt that the subject was a pharaoh, Auguste Mariette, the great French Egyptologist, suggested that perhaps the poor fellow had been captured while campaigning in the Sudan and castrated, with the effects visible in his statues—a suggestion that, as a recent historian put it, shows all "the vivid imagination one would expect of one of the librettists of *Aïda*."

In the sixth year of his reign, the young pharaoh made another, even more startling break. The Aten was his deity, not Amon; he was no more able to feel at ease in Thebes, under the shadow of Amon's awesome and sumptuous temples at Karnak and Luxor, than Martin Luther was in Rome. So he abandoned Thebes and set up a new capital at a place called today Tell el Amarna, some 250 miles downriver. He gave it the name Akhetaten, "the Horizon of the Aten," and at the same time changed his own name from Amenhotep to Akhenaten, "the Effective Spirit of the Aten." The Aten, in other words, was to be the official god of the land.

We know the new city better than any other in Egypt because after Akhenaten died in dishonor it was abandoned, to lie forgotten and undisturbed under a blanket of sand until archaeology began its resurrection at the end of the nineteenth century. Though Akhenaten's enemies had sown destruction with religious zeal, enough was left to reveal a well-planned complex. At its heart was a great temple to the Aten, which, in dramatic contrast to Amon's, was open, bathed in the sun's light. Surrounding it were the royal palace, administration buildings, an elegant residential section for members of the court, a humbler area for the rank and file, workshops, and so on. The cliffs roundabout were honeycombed with elaborate tombs; we have already described the housing project set up for the men engaged in cutting them.

In his new capital Akhenaten was free to worship as he liked. A hymn, presumably from his own hand, was found inscribed on the wall of a tomb belonging to one of his high officials. In it the king addresses his new god, in lofty and fervent phrases. It reveals a vision of a brave new world in which a single deity would replace the swarm that inhabited Egypt, above all would replace Amon. Reliefs from Amarna show the Aten with rays that end in hands stretching downward toward Akhenaten and his family, while any courtiers who are about bow reverently and humbly. Akhenaten, in other words, prayed to the Aten, and everyone else prayed to Akhenaten; there was no god but the one god, and Akhenaten was the sole entrée to him. At some point Akhenaten translated his egocentric monotheism into effective action: he sent men forth armed with mallets and chisels to strike out the offending name of Amon wherever they found it, whether on vast temples or tiny scarabs, whether in the heart of Thebes or deep in the Sudan. He even had them strike out such terms as "the gods."

Since most of what we know about Akhenaten's career comes from the archaeological record and very little from inscriptions or archives—we have a limited amount of such material from Egypt in general, and in the great heretic's case, whatever there was must have been systematically destroyed—the most obvious manifestation of his revolutionary regime is its art, the style that produced with such dramatic suddenness the monumentally ugly and distorted statues in his temple to the Aten. The Amarna style, as it is called, since the new capital was where it reached full bloom, is characterized by a departure from Egypt's rigid artistic ways toward a greater freedom and naturalism: the artists show figures in lifelike movement, in natural groupings, in easy poses. Actually, the beginnings of this art predate Akhenaten, for a certain amount of naturalism had made its appearance during the reigns of his predecessors; now, however, it comes strikingly to the fore. Poses and

Akhenaten and Nefertiti make offerings to the sun disk Aten. The deity sheds on them its rays, shown tipped with human hands. Akhenaten is portrayed not with the trim athletic figure traditionally given to the pharaoh in Egyptian art but with potbelly, big buttocks, and spindly shanks. (Relief from Tell el Amarna, now in the Cairo Museum.)

Akhenaten's daughters lolling on cushions. The painter gives them the same elongated skull as their father's and puts them in an informal pose typical of "Amarna" art. (Wall painting from Tell el Amarna, now in the Ashmolean Museum, Oxford.)

movements that artists previously had reserved only for minor figures—for dwarfs, dancers, yokels—are now given to the king and his family. Instead of the traditional static and formal court scenes, we get representations of the king munching on a bone or nuzzling his children, the queen dandling them on her lap, a pair of princesses lounging on cushions. Instead of a traditional heroic pharaoh, we get Akhenaten as he presumably looked, eggheaded, potbellied, spindly shanked. But the artists swiftly move from naturalism to mannerism—they give the whole family the very same set of characteristics. And the royal family's portraits in turn set a fashion: members of the court dutifully instruct their painters and sculptors to make them look like the pharaoh. These grotesqueries are the unmistakable mark of the years of the great heresy. As might be expected, Akhenaten's successors ostentatiously returned to Egypt's traditional artistic as well as religious ways.

Besides art, another source of information about the nature of the heresy is the hymn by Akhenaten mentioned above. In it the king addresses the Aten as the sole god, creator of all life, protector of the whole world:

> Thou appearest beautifully on the horizon of heaven,
> Thou living Aten, the beginning of life!
> When thou art risen on the eastern horizon,
> Thou hast filled every land with thy beauty.
> Thou art gracious, great, glistening, and high over every land;
> Thy rays encompass the lands to the limit of all that thou hast made:
> As thou art Re, thou reachest to the end of them;
> (Thou) subduest them (for) thy beloved son [Akhenaten].
> Though thou art far away, thy rays are on earth;
> Though thou art in their faces, no one knows thy going.
>
> When thou settest in the western horizon,
> The land is in darkness, in the manner of death.
> They sleep in a room, with heads wrapped up,
> Nor sees one eye the other.
> All their gods which are under their heads might be stolen.
> (But) they would not perceive (it).
> Every lion is come forth from his den;
> All creeping things, they sting.
> Darkness is a shroud, and the earth is in stillness,
> For he who made them rests in his horizon.
>
> At daybreak, when thou arisest on the horizon,
> When thou shinest as the Aten by day,
> Thou drivest away the darkness and givest thy rays.
> The Two Lands are in festivity every day,
> Awake and standing upon (their) feet,
> For thou hast raised them up.
> Washing their bodies, taking (their) clothing,

Their arms are (raised) in praise at thy appearance.
All the world, they do their work. . . .

Creator of seed in women,
Thou who makest fluid into man,
Who maintainest the son in the womb of his mother,
Who soothest him with that which stills his weeping,
Thou nurse (even) in the womb,
Who givest breath to sustain all that he has made!
When he descends from the womb to breathe
On the day when he is born,
Thou openest his mouth completely,
Thou suppliest his necessities. . . .

How manifold it is, what thou hast made!
They are hidden from the face (of man).
O sole god, like whom there is no other!
Thou didst create the world according to thy desire,
Whilst thou wert alone:
All men, cattle, and wild beasts,
Whatever is on earth, going upon (its) feet,
And what is on high, flying with its wings.

The hymn has justly been compared for depth of feeling and beauty
of expression with the Psalms. And it has frequently been pointed out
how not only the thought but even the wording is so closely paralleled
in the 104th Psalm. For example, the lines

How manifold it is, what thou hast made . . .
Thou didst create the world according to thy desire

recall Psalm 104:24,

O Lord, how manifold are thy works!
In wisdom hast thou made them all,

while these,

When thou settest in the western horizon,
The land is in darkness, in the manner of death . . .

> Every lion is come forth from his den;
> All creeping things, they sting

recall Psalm 104:20–21,

> Thou makest darkness, and it is night,
> Wherein all the beasts of the field creep forth.
> The young lions roar after their prey.

One god, creator of all living things, of all beasts and all men—such a concept was as much a departure from traditional Egyptian religion as the Amarna style was from traditional art.

What manner of man was this so un-Egyptian Egyptian who found a need to launch a new direction in art, who had the vision to conceive of an exalted monotheism, the zeal to strike down a religion hallowed by time, the megalomania to set himself up as the sole intermediary between god and man? The question has teased Egyptologists ever since the strange interlude that he created in Egyptian history first came to be known. They have picked over all the scraps of information we have about him in an effort to come upon some cogent explanation. Unfortunately there are only a mere handful, of which most are more tantalizing than informative. And so, over the years, a whole series of Akhenatens have emerged, each reflecting the writer's predilections and prejudices.

James Henry Breasted, for decades the leading figure in Chicago's Oriental Institute, was enthralled by the revolutionary pharaoh. He idolized this "lonely idealist of the Fourteenth Century before Christ," endowing him with a sensitive love of light and of nature comparable to Ruskin's or Wordsworth's, with a universal humanitarianism comparable to Alexander the Great's, with a profound and creative religious vision. He was passionately convinced that Akhenaten, a "god-intoxicated" man, was the true father of monotheism, that his hymn was a direct source for the Hebrew psalmist. Breasted painted a picture of his hero that is absorbing and exhilarating—but so is *Aïda,* and with just about as much basis in fact.

Balancing Breasted's religious visionary is the political and social reformer conjured up by a school infected with Marxist ideals. Akhenaten's creation of a new god and his retirement from Thebes, in their view, were moves in a class struggle, with the idealistic pharaoh upholding the cause of those under the heel of the entrenched interests. Heading a group of self-made men, he challenged the traditional ruling families and the traditional ideology, only to fall before an alliance of the army and reactionary clergy, particularly the priesthood of Amon, which was frantically eager to regain its lost power and revenues. It is a script no less imaginative than Breasted's.

One side of Akhenaten that has exercised a particular fascination has been the grotesque appearance he made his portraitists record so carefully. Was it pure affectation on his part to have himself pictured that way? Or did he actually look like that? And if so, what effect did it have on his ideals, on his chosen activities, since obviously no one of such a physique could possibly cast himself in the role of a conqueror like Thutmose III or a hunter and athlete like Amenhotep II. This is a point on which doctors presumably might have something to say, and several of them did. They pointed out that there is a pituitary disorder called Fröhlich's syndrome that produces symptoms remarkably similar to the features visible in Akhenaten's portraits: distortion of the skull, excessive growth of the jaw, plumping out of the abdomen and buttocks and thighs, overly slender lower limbs, corpulence, and infantile genitalia, at times so embedded in fat as to be invisible. Another candidate offered is Klinefelter's syndrome, a congenital chromosomal abnormality that can produce similar features. Either sounds convincing—until we remember that victims of both these ailments are infertile, whereas Akhenaten presumably fathered at least six daughters. A few historians, determined to salvage the enticing medical explanation at any price, convinced themselves that, in the reliefs showing Akhenaten fondling his babes, the pharaoh doth protest too much; they suggest that his father, who was still collecting recruits for his harem when well on in years, may have solved the son's embarrassing position by doing the sexual honors for him. Not *Aïda,* in other words, but *Tobacco Road.*

In 1951 John Wilson, one of Breasted's successors at the Oriental

Institute, gave a reconstruction of Akhenaten's reign that emphasized its manifest connections with the mainstream of Egyptian history. As he saw it, Akhenaten was independent-minded and avant-garde, sensitively responsive to the new currents that had been generated by Egypt's transformation to an international power. A freer, more naturalistic movement in art had already begun during his father's reign, and he favored it. A movement had gotten under way to flavor the rigidly stiff and formal traditional language with more up-to-date expressions, foreign borrowings, even colloquialisms, and he favored that. Above all he favored a new way of religion.

This religion was by no means totally novel; indeed, many of its ideas and modes of expression had been current before his time and after his excommunication would live on for centuries and ultimately affect Hebrew literature. However, his particular version definitely put him at odds with the powerful clerical establishment of the prevailing church, Amon's.

When his father died, the young thinker was free to put into effect the ideas that he had been germinating. He now began to order his artists to use the style that we always associate with him, one which, though based on the naturalistic movement already well under way, pushed it to extremes—as we know from his own statements, he treasured truth above all, and it follows that he would seek truth in art, portrayals of himself as he actually looked, pictures of himself in scenes that actually took place. After six years at Thebes, stronghold of the priests of Amon, who must have bitterly opposed him, he gathered together a coterie of devoted adherents from families of no particular standing—they recorded in their tomb inscriptions their heartfelt thanks to the pharaoh for their rise from nothing—and transferred to a new capital where he could implement his revolutionary ideas undisturbed. But the tide began to set against him. Even his idyllic family life was affected: Nefertiti was banned from the main palace—we find her name erased there and replaced by her eldest daughter's—to a residence at the northern end of town. He decided upon his younger brother, Smenkhare, as heir apparent, married him to his eldest daughter, and used him as go-between for a compromise with his enemies—there is evidence that the young man returned to Thebes and resumed relations there with Amon. Nefertiti, however, remained stubbornly devoted to the cause of revolution, and she must have kept the boy Tutankhamen, who was in line to succeed to the throne after Smenkhare, in her clutches, for their names appear together in her new dwelling.

Eventually both Akhenaten and Smenkhare disappear from the scene, probably carried off by death; Tutankhamen ascends the throne, and, bowing to the forces about him, engineers a return to the *status quo ante*. This is a persuasive reconstruction—but still just a reconstruction, based largely on inference from a word here, a picture there, an erasure in another place, and so on.

One of the most assiduous students of Akhenaten and his reign is Cyril Aldred. In his most recent book devoted to the maverick king, he reviews comprehensively and in depth every bit of information available, offers only those conclusions he feels sure of, and is content to leave all other questions open. One conclusion he feels sure of is that Akhenaten suffered from no disease but chose to show himself with those curious characteristics for theological reasons—although he frankly admits he has no answer to the question of why the king chose those particular characteristics. He feels sure that Nefertiti died in the fourteenth year of the reign (1340 B.C.) and that was why her name was erased and replaced by her daughter's; she did not outlive Akhenaten, she never fell into disgrace. The striking out of Amon's name, which is usually placed early in the reign, belongs, Aldred holds, to the last years, just before 1336 B.C. This was a time when the king suffered the loss of many who were near and dear to him—the death of two daughters and a beloved son-in-law on top of Nefertiti's. These personal difficulties were compounded by bad news from abroad: Egypt's influence in Syria had almost vanished and its hold on central Palestine was threatened. As a consequence of all this, something in Akhenaten gave way and he unleashed his fury on Amon. Aldred, working with the same fragments of information as Wilson, makes them yield a considerably different story.

Ancient Egypt, with its age-old dedication to tradition, was no place

Nefertiti portrayed in the naturalistic style typical of "Amarna" art. (Bust from Tell el Amarna, now in the Cairo Museum.)

for mavericks. Akhenaten was the only one in the long list of its royalty, and his successors did their best to rewrite Egypt's records and leave him out. In the official list of pharaohs, Horemheb's first year begins right after Amenhotep III's last, neatly consigning to oblivion all the rulers tainted with heresy—Akhenaten, Smenkhare, Tutankhamen. It has been the Egyptologists who have resurrected Akhenaten, exhuming his capital from the sands, extracting remains of his buildings at Thebes from the walls of later structures for which they had been cannibalized, deciphering the inscriptions left by him and his officials, making what inferences they could from his portraits and court scenes. But, barring a phenomenal piece of luck, except for stray bits of information that archaeology may produce, we very likely will never know much more about him than we do now. And this means that the answer to the seductive question of what made him a maverick will forever remain guesswork. Was he an inspired visionary? convinced but misguided reformer? megalomaniac? madman? Take your pick—or, if you prefer, wait for further choices; that these will be forthcoming is the one thing about Akhenaten we may be sure of.

CHAPTER XI

The Afterlife

In the most ancient tombs found in the Valley of the Nile, dating back to the fourth millennium B.C., the deceased lie surrounded with food, drink, clothing, cosmetics, weapons, tools—in short, all the things they found useful when alive. Clearly the Egyptians' belief in a life beyond the grave that was a continuation in most important respects of the life they led on earth arose very early in their history.

During the flourishing days of the Old Kingdom, when the pharaoh's role as god on earth had not yet been diminished in any way, it was thought that immortality had been granted to him alone, and all others partook of it solely through him. Nobles had their tombs placed as near as possible to the royal one and proclaimed in inscriptions on the walls their dependence upon the pharaoh and the services they had performed for him; all this presumably ensured that they would go on being his agents after death as they had been in life. A similar path was open to lesser mortals: the pharaoh's servants, artisans, peasants, and other members of his household and estates who gained mention in the texts written in his tomb or inclusion in the scenes sculpted in it might count on serving him beyond the grave. Excavation has revealed some grim instances where servants and retainers were slaughtered and laid to rest alongside their dead masters or mistresses presumably to wait on them in the afterlife. They had the consolation that by burial in the same tomb they were assured a share in whatever immortality the fortunate deceased had earned.

However, by the Fifth Dynasty, when the pharaoh's status and authority had begun to slip, he inevitably lost his power as the sole holder of the key to eternal life. During the troubled period that began about 2150 B.C., when Egypt broke apart into little principalities under local rulers, the nobility gained increased standing and power, and nobles adopted for themselves the funeral rites and arrangements once limited to the royal blood: in other words, they held themselves to be in a position to gain immortality on their own, not vicariously. And there is good reason to believe that things went still further, that immortality was democratized, as it were, and every Egyptian in the land, high or humble, came to consider himself eligible for eternal life after death. This was certainly the case by Middle Kingdom times. Pedigree and the income that went with it gave a man a fine burial and an elaborate tomb, but such things meant only a higher degree of post-mortem comfort. Now prayers and rites and way of life were what gained one entrée to immortality, and these were at the disposal of everybody.

Above all there were the prayers and rites for the moment when each dead person stood in judgment before Osiris, god of the underworld. For a while after immortality was first opened up to others than the pharaoh and his family, there was a moral aspect to this judgment: the defendant had to prove he had lived righteously to gain eternal happiness. But the Egyptians in their practical way soon got around that: in New Kingdom times a complicated system of prayers, spells, incantations, and other such means was worked out that guaranteed a successful issue of the trial. The texts of these were written down on papyrus; a collection of them is what the Egyptologists have titled the Book of the Dead. The part that gave precise instructions on what to do when face to face with the awful judge was often placed between the legs of the corpse so that the deceased might have it for handy reference. It con-

Underworld scene picturing a crucial moment: the deceased, at the far left, looks on as his heart is weighed against a feather by Anubis, the jackal-headed god. (Illustration from Any's Book of the Dead, a papyrus document dating to the Nineteenth Dynasty, now in the British Museum.)

tained what has been called the negative confession, a detailed denial of the commission of sin. The key passage runs as follows:

What is said on reaching the Broad-Hall of the Two Justices [that is, the place where the underworld judgment was held] absolving [here follow the name and title of the deceased] of every sin which he has committed. . . .

I have not committed evil against men.

I have not mistreated cattle.

I have not committed sin in the place of truth [that is, a temple or burial ground]. . . .

I have not blasphemed a god.

I have not done violence to a poor man.

I have not done that which the gods abominate.

I have not defamed a slave to his superior.

I have not made (anyone) sick.

I have not made (anyone) weep.

I have not killed.

I have given no order to a killer.

I have not caused anyone suffering. . . .

I have not had sexual relations with a boy.

I have not defiled myself. . . .

I have not added to the weight of the balance.

I have not weakened the plummet of the scales.

I have not taken milk from the mouths of children.

I have not driven cattle away from their pasturage. . . .

I have not held up the water in its season [that is, denied flood waters to others].

I have not built a dam against running water. . . .

The denials to be made totaled thirty-six in all, but going through them was just the beginning. The defendant next had to convince forty-two jurors who bore such terrifying names as Breaker-of-Bones, Eater-of-Entrails, Embracer-of-Fire, and the like. He addressed them individually, denying a given sin before each, for example, "O Breaker-of-Bones . . . I have not told lies. . . . O Eater-of-Entrails . . . I have not practiced usury . . . O Embracer-of-Fire . . . I have not stolen." He followed this with a speech asserting how genuinely good he was and listing his charitable actions: "I have given bread to the hungry, water to the thirsty, clothing to the naked, and a ferryboat to him who was marooned," and more to the same effect. The instructions offering this rigmarole close with specific directions on procedure: "This spell is to be recited when one is clean and pure, clothed in (fresh) garments, shod with white sandals, painted with stibium [eye cosmetic], and anointed with myrrh, to whom cattle, fowl, incense, bread, beer, and vegetables have been offered."

Deluxe illustrated copies of the Book of the Dead have been found, and these reveal how the Egyptians pictured the scene. Osiris sits on his throne with, below him, fourteen assessors and a large set of scales. In one side is placed the defendant's heart, which the Egyptians conceived to be the seat of the mind and will. In the other is placed the symbol for *maat,* often just a feather. Anubis, the jackal god, supervises the weighing, and Thoth, patron deity of scribes, books the results. There was always the possibility that a heart might double-cross its owner at the critical moment, so the Book of the Dead contains prayers to circumvent such a contingency: "O my heart . . . set not thyself up to bear witness against me, speak not against me in the presence of the judges, cast not thy weight against me before the lord of the scales." Any judged guilty were turned over to a monster for annihilation. Since all Egyptians had access to these sure-fire spells and procedures, presumably there were few who had to fear such a fate.

Having passed judgment in Osiris's court, the deceased became one with Osiris (in Egyptian texts the dead are addressed as "the Osiris So-and-So"; it was the equivalent of our "the late John Doe"). He was then free to take up his eternal existence. The Egyptians were rather hazy about what this was. In Old Kingdom times the pharaoh was thought to ascend to the heavens and join the gods there. When the worship of Re became important, he was conceived of as accompanying the sun in the circuit of the sky during the day and journeying through the starry underworld at night; this is why royal burial included solar boats, for transport during these aerial voyages. Later the dead were thought of as inhabiting the underworld; some illustrated funerary papyri show them happily working away there. The commonest view was that the dead passed their existence in the tomb, with, however, opportunity for forays out of it. The Egyptians believed that human beings were made up of a body inhabited by a *ka,* a life-force, universal and indestructible, that emanated from god, and a *ba,* more or less a soul in our sense, which had the power to leave the body temporarily by way of dreams and visions. Death took place when both these forces deserted the body. By preserving the body through mummification and providing for it a "house of eternity," as tombs were called, the Egyptian made it possible for a *ka* and *ba* to return and take up their wonted residence and thereby restore the dead to life. The *ba* even retained its mobility— illustrations in the papyrus texts picture it as a bird with human head— enabling it to leave the mummy and revisit the haunts of its former existence.

But life after death was not necessarily a static residence in the dark of a tomb varied by excursions of one's *ba*. As noted above, the Egyptians, with their customary elasticity of thought, also conceived of an underworld where things went on just as they had on earth, where men plowed, sowed, reaped, irrigated, where they were even subject to a corvée, for, just as the pharaohs conscripted their subjects for work on national projects, so did the gods conscript the dead for similar services in the underworld. To spare themselves such arduous labor in eternity, the Egyptians stocked their tombs with *ushebtis,* "answerers," little faience or pottery figurines that were magically able to answer to the call and do the work in the dead man's place. These were usually inscribed with just the owner's name and rank but sometimes with detailed instructions: "The Osiris So-and-So, he says, 'O *ushebti,* if the Osiris So-and-So is counted, called by name, and summoned to do all the tasks . . . in the necropolis, as a man does them in his own behalf, to make the fields fertile, to make water flow through the channels, to carry the sand from east to west or from west to east, to pull up the weeds, like a man on his own behalf, you must say, "I will do it, here am I." ' " The figurines were even equipped with their appropriate implements—picks and hammers for the masons and carpenters, hoes for the peasants, yokes for the carriers of sand and water, large and small baskets for other carriers.

The Egyptians, as we have several times observed, were by nature buoyant, optimistic, and confident, and their view of the afterlife reflects this: throughout most of their history they conceived of it as something to be enjoyed, certainly not to be looked on with foreboding. Being at the same time pragmatic and material minded, they indulged in no fancies about its being a better world. As they saw it, death meant a continuation of one's life on earth, a continuation that, with the appropriate precautions of proper burial, prayer, and ritual, would include only the best parts of life on earth—nothing to fear, but on the other hand, nothing to want to hurry out of this world for. This attitude lasted from Old Kingdom times right up to the end of the Nineteenth Dynasty, about 1200 B.C., when change becomes noticeable. Pictures and texts in tombs from this time on no longer concern themselves with life on earth. The pictures cease portraying the deceased serenely contemplating the bustling life on his estates, and concentrate morbidly on the making of the mummy, the funeral, the judgment before Osiris, the demons the dead will see, and other aspects of death. The texts give up autobiography in favor of magical recipes for getting along in the life beyond the grave. This shift of emphasis is one of the distinctive features that mark Egypt's descent toward the religion-haunted, superstitious, ritualistic nation it was to become by the time Herodotus and other Greek and Roman authors wrote down their impressions.

But the shift did not occur until the very end of the period we are concerned with. Throughout most of the New Kingdom the Egyptians prepared for their entry into the next world with calm and confidence. It was an occupation that absorbed their time and resources for most of their life, since they were unable to rest easy until assured that the place of their final repose and its furnishings were ready. In *The Story of Sinuhe,* a Middle Kingdom tale of an official who went into exile but in his old age was recalled by the pharaoh in time to end his days happily in the fatherland, Sinuhe recounts the crowning joy of his homecoming:

There was constructed for me a pyramid-tomb of stone in the midst of the pyramid-tombs. The stone-masons who hew a pyramid-tomb took over its ground-area. The outline-draftsmen designed in it; the chief sculptors carved in it; and the overseers of works who are in the necropolis made it their concern. Its necessary materials were made from all the outfittings which are placed at a tomb-shaft. Mortuary priests were given to me. There was made for me a necropolis garden, with fields in it formerly (extending) as far as the town, like that which is done for a chief courtier. My statue was overlaid with gold, and its skirt was of fine gold. It was his majesty who had it made.

During the Old Kingdom, a pharaoh's burial place was a whole complex of which the pyramid was simply the most prominent part. There was also a mortuary temple for holding services for the dead and a causeway leading to a "Valley Temple" placed near the bank of the river. Roundabout clustered the mastabas, the flat-roofed rectangular buildings where his courtiers were buried to guarantee them a share in the pharaonic immortality. Pyramid tombs continued into the Middle Kingdom, and, as Sinuhe's story shows, they served notables as well as kings. The New Kingdom brought in a decisive change. Burial structures above ground, veritable signposts for would-be plunderers, were abandoned in favor of tombs cut deep into the rock of the cliffs that lined the river. The Egyptians cherished the hope that these could be safely sealed off from intruders—a vain hope, since every one, with the single haphazard exception of Tutankhamen's, was robbed in antiquity. Thutmose I was the first to carve out a tomb for himself in the Valley of the Kings at Thebes, and all the subsequent pharaohs of the Eighteenth, Nineteenth, and Twentieth Dynasties followed suit. Each royal tomb consists of a series of subterranean corridors that burrow into the hillside to end in a chamber where the body was placed. On the walls were no scenes of life on earth but of Re making his voyage through the demon-infested realms of the underworld; these presumably were a guide for the deceased in his own journeys there. Other pictures show the pharaoh accompanied by various deities. The tomb was sealed at the entrance, for it was for the dead alone, never intended to be visited. The mortuary temple, where priests would carry on, presumably forever, the services for the dead king, lay a good distance away in the plain that flanked the Nile. Tombs for the nobility were also rock-cut, and the cliffs along the west bank at Thebes are honeycombed with them. They, however, were to be visited, and so a prominent feature was an antechamber carved into the face of the cliff where visitors could enter and view on the walls paintings showing the deceased in characteristic activities: watching the peasants at work, supervising the artisans of the king's workshops, being received in audience by the king, hunting, and so on. From the antechamber a shaft led to the burial chamber, but once the funeral had taken place and the body had been laid to rest, this was closed off to all further access.

The construction of a tomb was the chief step in the preparations for death, but by no means the only one. The chamber had to be furnished and stocked fully with supplies; the deceased, after all, since they were going to go on living, would need all they had needed on earth, and plenty of it, inasmuch as their subterranean existence was to be a long one. In Tutankhamen's tomb the excavators found couches, beds, chariots, boats, boxes, chests, all kinds of chairs, all kinds of weapons, walking sticks, games, metal and stone vessels, dishes, a variety of food. Above all there was the coffin to be readied and the four receptacles, the so-called Canopic jars, that would hold the organs removed from the body. Next to the building of the tomb, the Egyptians' major concern was the carving of the coffin, the elaborately decorated stone box in which the mummy would be placed. Tutankhamen had multiple coffins, each fitting inside the other, three inner ones of gold as well as the stone sarcophagus.

Even after death there was a lengthy operation to be carried out—the embalming of the corpse. Herodotus, that inquisitive and sharp-eyed tourist, poked his nose into the undertakers' establishments and has left us an invaluable description of how mummies were prepared:

The embalmers, when a body is brought to them, show the people who have brought it samples in painted wood resembling embalmed corpses, the finest grade . . . a second grade that is inferior and cheaper, and a third grade that is the cheapest. After making their explanations, they find out from the people which way they want the corpse prepared. When agreement has been reached about price, the people depart, leaving the embalmers to go to work. The finest grade of embalming is as follows. First, by means of a bent iron instrument inserted in the nostrils they extract the brains; some they extract, some they flush out with liquid pharmaceuticals. Next, with a sharp stone knife they make an incision in the flank and empty the whole abdominal cavity, washing and rinsing it first with palm wine and then rinsing with an infusion of ground spices. Then they fill the cavity with pure ground myrrh and casia and all other spices, except frankincense, and sew up the incision. Having completed this operation, they put the body in natron, keeping it completely covered, for seventy days; the treatment with natron cannot be extended for any more time than that. When the seventy days are up, they wash the body and wrap it all up in bandages of fine linen smeared with gum, which the Egyptians use in place of glue. Then the deceased's relatives take it over and give orders to make a wooden case in human shape. When this is ready, they put the body in it and, fastening the cover, set it in the tomb chamber standing upright against a wall.

This is the most expensive way to embalm a corpse. For those who choose the middle grade to avoid expense, the preparation is as follows. By means of syringes containing oil of cedar they fill up the abdominal cavity: no incision is made nor is the cavity emptied; they insert the syringes through the anus and then stop it up. The treatment with natron is carried on for the appropriate number of days, and on the last day they empty the cavity of the oil that had been injected. The oil is so powerful that it dissolves the stomach and guts and brings these out with it. The natron has dissolved the flesh, so all that is left of the corpse is the skin and bones. When this operation is complete, they return the body without doing anything further to it. The third grade of mummification is for people with little money. They cleanse the abdominal cavity with a purge, put the body in natron for seventy days, and then hand it over to be carried away. Wives of men of standing or women who are beautiful and important are not turned over to the embalmers immediately after death but only after a delay of three to four days. This is done in order to prevent the embalmers from having intercourse with them. For it is said that one was caught having intercourse with a newly deceased woman; a fellow worker reported the act.

Examination of actual mummies has confirmed much of what Herodotus says. The key element in the process was the burying in natron—the bodies were, in effect, dried out the way fish are dried out by salting. Salt would have done just as well as natron, but in Egyptian eyes natron was the purifying agent par excellence, and by using it they produced a body ritually clean as well as mummified. The period of seventy days was a matter of religious belief; the number could just as well have been less. The brain and organs (save the heart and kidneys) were generally removed. It is impossible to confirm or deny his statement that in cheaper burials the intestines were cleaned out, but here again it would seem an eminently reasonable step—although whatever agent was used, it surely would not have had the powerful effect Herodotus ascribes to it. No mummies have been found with the incision sewed up; that may have been a short-lived practice limited to Herodotus' own day. His key omission is the use of resin, for Egyptian embalmers applied it liberally. Often the abdominal cavity was filled with a solid mass of resin or with linen or sawdust soaked in resin; often the body and the bandages were smeared with it—though there are cases of smearing with gum (probably from the acacia, a tree that was common in ancient Egypt), as Herodotus reports.

Those who had to be content with the cheaper grades of embalming had to be equally content with cheaper types of burial. Unused or abandoned tombs or large caverns were frequently turned into common graves and stacked with coffins, one on top of the other, from floor to ceiling; the tools, clothes, ornaments, *ushebtis,* and so on that the dead needed were stuffed into the coffin. The Egyptian potter's field was an area in the midst of the necropolis where paupers' mummies, wrapped in coarse cloth, were tossed one upon the other with but a thin layer of sand separating them.

When the mummy was finally ready, the funeral could take place. The ceremony for a departed Egyptian noble was an imposing affair. There was a long cortege consisting of the family, friends, servants, and a squad of hired mourners; the last, usually women with mud-smeared faces, bared breasts, and torn garments, kept up an obbligato of groaning, keening, head smiting, and other demonstrations of grief. The servants were loaded down with all that was to be deposited in the tomb, from garlands of flowers to massive pieces of furniture. The sarcophagus, in a sumptuous catafalque on a sled, was drawn along by men and oxen. All proceeded down to the waterfront; there boats were waiting to ferry everybody across to the west bank, where the necropolis lay. On landing at the other side, the procession reformed and made its way across the flat plain of the bank and up into the area where the tombs were cut in cliffs. Here the priests went through a last ritual designed to restore to the corpse its power of movement and its senses, the mourning hit a crescendo, and the file of servants descended into the tomb to deposit what they were carrying, each item in its appointed place. Everyone finally withdrew, the masons walled up the passage to the tomb chamber, and all repaired to a spot in front of the tomb or nearby to enjoy the funeral feast.

The funeral was just the first of a series of services on behalf of the deceased that were to go on, theoretically, until the end of time. People of property would leave endowments whose income was to ensure forever and ever the recital of the proper prayers, the placing of offerings on the table in front of the tomb, and other necessary rituals. The Old Kingdom pharaohs, in order to support their huge burials, gave over to these endowments enormous properties; one of the causes of the downfall of the Old Kingdom was the withdrawal of such vast amounts of land from the normal economy to support nonproductive funerary purposes. The prayers and rituals were to be daily, at the very least on important holidays. But such things depend upon the living, and the living tend to have short memories. Family visits to make prayers and offerings grew further and further apart. The priests involved in the mortuary contracts would get lax or would sign on to care for so many tombs that they could not possibly find time for all of them and would skip days or subcontract out to lesser priests. The inevitable result was neglect, and neglected tombs were an invitation to robbers. The time came when, as a cynic writing as early as the period between the Old and Middle Kingdom put it, the rich man was no better off than the hard-working poor man who fell dead during a job: "They who build in granite and who hew out chambers in a pyramid . . . as soon as the builders have become gods [that is, have died], their offering-stones are as bare, for lack of a survivor, as (those of) the weary ones, the dead on the dike."

CHAPTER XII

Travel

"I reached Elephantine [at the First Cataract], as I had been ordered. . . . I returned by the route I took out [that is, sailed back down the river]. I moored at Abydos. I left my name in the place of the god Osiris." So runs an inscription of the chamberlain of Amenemhet II, who ruled about 1875 B.C. Amenemhet had sent him on some assignment; he had used Egypt's commonest form of travel, boat on the Nile, and he had taken advantage of the occasion to stop en route at Abydos and do what every Egyptian yearned to do, leave a memorial in the sacred precinct of Osiris there. Year in and year out the pharaoh's men—officials, representatives, agents, couriers—shuttled back and forth between the capital and the various parts of the kingdom. With a government as highly centralized as Egypt's, it could not be otherwise.

Nor were their travels confined within the borders. As early as the First Dynasty, the Egyptians were extracting copper and turquoise from the hills of Sinai, and this produced a steady flow of traffic across the eastern desert; we quoted above the words of an official who had to make the journey in the brutal heat of early summer. Some forty miles northwest of Cairo lies the Wadi Natrun, a prime source of the natron essential for mummification, purificatory rites, and other vital services,

so there was heavy traffic in this direction as well. To the south the pharaoh's dispatch riders kept him in touch with what was going on in the
gold mines of Nubia, while his trade representatives ventured even farther south. A certain noble named Harkhuf, who lived toward the end
of the Old Kingdom, was responsible for garnering products from sub-
Saharan Africa. As he reports in a short autobiography he had carved on
his tomb, he made three trips deep into the Sudan. The first was "to
open up the way to this country. I did it in seven months and brought
back from it all kinds of good and rare presents. . . . His Majesty sent me
a second time. . . . I set forth from the First Cataract . . . and returned . . .
in the space of eight months. I returned and brought presents from this
country in very great quantity. . . . His majesty sent me a third time. . . .
I returned with 300 asses loaded with incense, ebony, oil, leopard skins,
elephant tusks, boomerangs, and all good products."

It is unlikely that Harkhuf made his way to the haunts of leopard and
elephant or the lands where incense and ebony came from. He very
likely got no farther than the Second or Third Cataract; here there must
have been a trading post, the end of a trail that started far to the south.

One area that the Egyptians early established contact with was Ethiopia and Somalia, or Punt as they called it. From here they drew myrrh
and frankincense, two invaluable imports; the first was essential for
perfumes and drugs, and the second smoked on altars throughout the
kingdom. The area could be reached either overland by caravan—
which is the way Harkhuf got the incense he refers to—or by ship down
the Red Sea. The water route was interrupted during the years that
Egypt suffered under the Hyksos invasion. Queen Hatshepsut re-
established it and considered the act so important that on her tomb she
included an account, complete with illustrations, of the expedition she
had dispatched. We see five slender galleys, three still under sail and two
that have already doused sail and are preparing to tie up; the lines of
their hulls are so sleek that they seem far more suited to the placid Nile
than to boisterous open water. We see an Egyptian representative offer
the traditional objects of barter—necklaces, hatchets, daggers—to the
king and queen and their family; behind them, surrounded by palms,

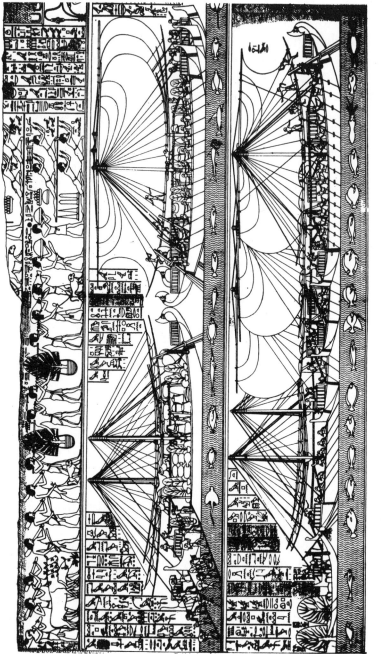

Scene at a port in Punt: stevedores load one of the ships of Hatshepsut's fleet with local products (cattle, myrrh trees bagged for transplanting, pet monkeys). Another, already loaded, gets under way. (Drawing of a relief on the tomb of Hatshepsut at Deir el-Bahari.)

rise the round huts with domed roofs of the village they rule. We see a line of Puntite stevedores loading the vessels with the country's products, piling the decks high with timber, ivory, hides, cattle, incense, even a cluster of live incense trees, their roots carefully bagged, for transplanting. There were souvenirs too—native spears, monkeys, dogs, and, as the text informs us, "a southern panther alive, captured for Her Majesty." The scenes are captioned, down to minute details; for example, the pilot of one of the vessels calls out, "Hard to port!" while "Watch your step!" is inscribed over the stevedores.

Seaborne traffic to the north was heavier than to the south since the commodities from there were bulkier and the volume of trade greater. As early as Old Kingdom times Egyptian ships were sailing to the coast of Lebanon to take on cargoes of timber, resin, and other forest products.

For a land confined, as Egypt was, in the Valley of the Nile, the river was the natural means of communication. And it was a most convenient one to boot, for not only was it navigable up to the First Cataract, but the prevailing wind blows from the north—in other words, opposite to the direction of flow. Boatmen were able to use the current one way and the wind the other. They would drift downstream with hardly more crew on duty than lookouts in the bows and helmsmen on the poop to handle the steering oars. For the trip upstream they would raise the sail. The Egyptian sail was made of woven papyrus fibers and was stretched by a boom along the foot as well as by a yard along the head; in Old Kingdom times boatmen preferred a sail far taller than wide, but by the Middle Kingdom they had switched to just the opposite, one far broader than tall. Since sailing upriver could be a slow business, vessels carrying passengers or dispatches were most often galleys, of a special Egyptian design for use on the river. The galley had slender lines, long overhangs fore and aft, and was propelled by a line of rowers on each side who worked short oars with a choppy stroke that dipped the blades deep into the water. On some stretches where neither current nor wind was particularly helpful, or along canals where the current was negligible and there was not room enough to sail, towed boats were employed, pulled by a line of haulers trudging along a towpath.

Nile craft ran the gamut of size, shape, and looks. In the waters along the banks and in the canals branching off from them were swarms of canoes made of bundles of papyrus reeds lashed together. In the mainstream of the river were the ponderous freighters; these were constructed of short pieces of planking—the best that tree-starved Egypt could offer—skillfully joined together. They hauled flocks of cattle, sacks of grain, jars of oil and beer and wine—everything right up to huge blocks of stone destined for some building site or some sculptor's work area. A picture on Hatshepsut's tomb shows the twin obelisks that she set up in the temple at Karnak being transported downriver from the quarries at Aswan; the giant shafts lie, butt to butt, on the deck of a Brobdingnagian barge towed by a flotilla of 27 tugs powered by 864 oarsmen. Lording it over the workaday craft were the handsome galleys assigned to government officials. And even these were put in the shade by the gorgeously decorated vessels that during Amon's festivals carried his sacred image to Luxor or across the river. His festivals, as a matter of fact, marked the apogee of traffic on the Nile, for just about everything that would float was pressed into service to accommodate the throngs headed for Thebes to enjoy the spectacle. We cited earlier Herodotus' description of the vast conclave that came by water to the festival for the goddess Bast; Amon's attracted even more.

Travel by land went mostly along roads that followed the lines of the ubiquitous irrigation canals. The canals were constantly being cleaned out; the mud dredged from the bottom was piled up alongside to form a protective dike, and the top of the dike was smoothed and packed to form a road. Roads so fashioned were most often little more than paths, so the Egyptians had scant use for carts or wagons. They either walked or rode donkeys. In Egypt, as throughout the rest of the ancient Near East, the donkey was the standard beast of burden. Camels, although known, were not in common use until as late as Ptolemaic times. Horses were for chariots, and chariots, aside from hunting and war, were for pleasure rides, not serious travel.

Sooner or later persons walking or riding came upon a canal they had to get over, and this could pose a problem since the Egyptians did not go in for bridges. If the crossing was short and there were no crocodiles about, they would swim. Otherwise they would search out a ferryman. Those rich enough to own their own boats were expected, as an act of charity, to give whoever wanted it a hitch across. As we noted above, the rigmarole the deceased were instructed to utter in front of Osiris at the last judgment included the asseveration that they had "given . . . a ferryboat to him who was marooned." For crossing the Nile there were public ferries available. Strabo, the Greek geographer, who visited Egypt toward the end of the first century B.C., reports that the inhabitants of Dendera had no hesitation in swimming the river, crocodiles and all, but he also makes it clear that they were the only ones who boasted such sang-froid.

When Harkhuf the royal chamberlain went to the Sudan, he unquestionably had with him a squad of scribes to inventory the goods he acquired. Scribes accompanied Hatshepsut's expedition to Punt, the shipments of gold from Nubia, of copper from Sinai, of natron from the western desert. So well traveled were Egypt's scribes that there arose among them some who became interested in travel for its own sake—history's first tourists. We are aware of their existence thanks to a tourist characteristic that has not changed in thousands of years—the urge to leave one's name in the places one has visited. In Middle Kingdom tombs archaeologists have found the graffiti of New Kingdom scribes who, as they state, "came to see the tomb." Many of the scribblers, just as today, were content merely to leave their names: "The scribe Pennewet," "The scribe Wia," and the like. Others had more to say. "Hadnakhte, scribe of the treasury," reads a graffito written about 1250 B.C. on a wall in a chapel connected with Djoser's pyramid, ". . . came to make an excursion and amuse himself on the west of Memphis, together with his brother, Panakhti, scribe of the Vizier." On a wall of the chapel to the goddess Sekhmet in the pyramid complex at Abu Sir is a graffito, of more or less the same date, to the effect that the scribe Ptah-Emwe and his father, also a scribe, "came to contemplate the shadow of the pyramids after having been to present offerings to Sekhmet." They were like the tourist of today who goes to a famous cathedral both to light a candle and enjoy the architecture. Scribes were such regular visitors to Egypt's monuments that they worked out a formula for their graffiti which, being an unimaginative and conservative lot, they used with scant variation for hundreds of years. "Scribe So-and-So," it goes, "of clever fingers, came to see the temple of the blessed King So-and-So." Despite the reference to their "clever fingers," that is, their skill with a pen, their performance could on occasion leave much to be desired, to judge from an irate blast on a chapel wall in Djoser's complex:

The scribe of clever fingers came, a clever scribe without his equal among any men of Memphis, the scribe Amenemhet. I say: Explain to me these words [presumably some illiterate graffiti he saw]. My heart is sick when I see the work of their hands. . . . It is like the work of a woman who has no mind; would that we had someone who could have denounced them before ever they entered in to see the Temple. I have seen a scandal; they are no scribes such as Thoth has enlightened!

Toward the end of the nineteenth century a papyrus was discovered that contains a unique record of travel, a report drawn up about 1100 B.C. by a priest named Wenamon of a business trip he had made. It is our earliest detailed account of a voyage, and the bald, intensely personal narrative gives the events a vivid reality.

Wenamon, attached to the temple of Amon at Thebes, was selected by the high priest to go to Byblos in Lebanon in order to purchase a cargo of timber cut from the famous cedars; it was needed for the construction of the ceremonial barge to be used in the annual festival. Wenamon made his way down to the delta, where passage was arranged for him on a vessel bound for Syria. On April 20 his ship shoved off, sailed down to the river's mouth, and "embarked on the great Syrian sea."

The first port of call was a town named Dor, a little to the south of Carmel, which had been established about a century earlier by a tribe of sea raiders called the Tjeker. Here Wenamon suffered catastrophe: as he tells it in his businessman's language, "A man of my ship ran away, having stolen one [vessel] of gold [amounting] to five *deben* [about 1.2

pounds], four vessels of silver amounting to twenty *deben,* a sack of silver—eleven *deben.* [Total of what] he [stole]: five *deben* of gold, thirty-one *deben* [about 7.5 pounds] of silver." The poor fellow had been robbed of every penny he had, his travel allowance as well as the cash he had been given to pay for the lumber.

Wenamon tried to bully the prince of Dor into making up the loss but got nowhere. The prince, however, promised to make an investigation and graciously offered Wenamon hospitality while he awaited the results. After nine fruitless days had gone by, Wenamon got impatient and left. At this point the papyrus is tattered, and we can merely guess from scraps of sentences at what happened. He seems to have continued on his way and at some point solved his desperate dilemma with a desperate expedient: the priest of Amon held up some Tjeker and took thirty *deben* of silver from them. "[I have seized] your silver," he explained to his victims, "and it will stay with me [until] you find [mine or the thief] who stole it! Even though you have not stolen, I shall take it."

Wenamon's troubles, as it turned out, had just begun. The moment he arrived at Byblos, the harbormaster greeted him with a curt order from Zakar-Baal, the ruling prince: "Get out (of) my harbor!" Probably the Tjeker had sent ahead a wanted-for-robbery notice, and since they were neighbors to the south and formidable sea raiders as well, the prince was anxious to maintain good relations with them. But Wenamon was not an easy man to discourage. For twenty-nine days he hung around the harbor, even though every morning the harbormaster dutifully brought him the same message. Zakar-Baal apparently went no further than that. He wanted to stay on the right side of his touchy neighbors, but at the same time he was reluctant to lose a sale. So he compromised by issuing an ultimatum and doing nothing to enforce it. However, when Wenamon showed unmistakable signs of giving up and returning to Egypt, Zakar-Baal abruptly changed his tactics and summoned the envoy for an interview. "I found him," Wenamon writes, "sitting (in) his upper room, with his back turned to a window, so that the waves of the great Syrian sea broke against the back of his head." Most unusual language for Wenamon, who elsewhere limits himself to an unvarnished tale; the scene must have burned itself into his memory. After much discussion Zakar-Baal agreed to grant Wenamon an extension of time so that he could send to Egypt for a cargo of goods to help defray the cost of the timber; obviously the money he had stolen fell far short of what was needed.

Forty-eight days passed before the shipment arrived, a rich agglomeration of prized Egyptian exports: papyrus rolls, linen, hides, gold, silver, and other items. Zakar-Baal ordered the felling of the trees to start immediately, and finally, eight months after Wenamon had left Thebes, the timber lay on the beach cut and stacked, ready for loading. At this point, just when things looked brightest, eleven war galleys suddenly hove into the harbor bearing an ultimatum for the prince: "Arrest Wenamon! Don't let a ship of his (go) to the land of Egypt!" The galleys were manned by Tjeker raiders; they were demanding justice for the thirty *deben* of silver that had been stolen from them months and months before. Wenamon did the only thing he could under the circumstances: "I sat down and wept," he reports. Zakar-Baal, either because he genuinely felt sorry or did not want to let a profitable sale slip through his fingers, tried to console the poor Egyptian. His method has a curiously modern ring: he sent him a ram, two jugs of wine, and a girl.

Whatever pleasure Wenamon got out of his food, drink, and girl must have swiftly evaporated when he heard Zakar-Baal's decision the next morning. It was another of the prince's cagey compromises. "I cannot arrest the messenger of Amon inside my land," he told the Tjeker, "but let me send him away, and you go after him to arrest him." He was going to discharge his obligation to Egypt—and at the same time save his sale—by not turning Wenamon over to the Tjeker; and he was going to avoid offending the Tjeker by sending Wenamon out of his jurisdiction where they could lay their hands on him—with a bit of a head start to give him a chance. Wenamon no doubt had his views on what chance vessels chartered for hauling timber had of escaping from a crack squadron of sea raiders.

The next portion of the narrative is tantalizingly bad. "So he loaded me in," Wenamon writes, "and he sent me away from there. . . . And the wind cast me on the land of Alashiya [Cyprus]." In other words, the wind took him in a direction almost opposite to what he wanted. Quite likely it was one of the southeasterly gales that are common off the coast of Syria. It may have been his salvation: a heavy cargo ship would have a chance of riding it out, but not a light galley, and this may explain why the Tjeker apparently never pursued him. Possibly they figured the storm would save them the job.

But Wenamon had fled the frying pan just to fall into the fire: at Alashiya a group of natives descended upon him and hustled him off to kill him. Pirate incursions were chronic along all the coasts of that area at the time; these particular people no doubt had suffered their share, and they may have welcomed Wenamon's advent as a chance to turn the tables. Wenamon was able to force his way to the palace of the local ruler, a princess, and "met her as she was going out of one house of hers and going into another. . . . I greeted her, and I said to the people who were standing near her, 'Isn't there one of you who understands Egyptian?' And one of them said, 'I understand (it).' So I said to him, 'Tell my lady—' " but the speech is unimportant and doubtless represents what, years later at his desk in Thebes, he reckoned he ought to have said rather than what a wet, exhausted, and frightened wayfarer actually did say. The important point is that the princess listened. "She had the people summoned and they stood there," writes Wenamon, "and she said to me, 'Spend the night—' " and here the papyrus abruptly breaks off. We will never know how he got home or whether the timber arrived safely. We only know that he did get back, or else this report would never have been written down.

CHAPTER XIII

Egypt under Non-Egyptians

After the close of the Twentieth Dynasty around 1075 B.C. Egypt's days as a unified country under Egyptian kings gradually came to an end. By the middle of the eighth century B.C. centralized rule was a thing of the past; the land had broken up into a cluster of states and principalities. Nubia to the south, once subject to Egypt but now a prosperous and powerful independent nation, took advantage of the situation and mounted an invasion; its armies were successful, and for a century a dynasty of Nubian pharaohs sat on the throne of Egypt. Their advent brought no great changes, for the Nubians had been so thoroughly Egyptianized that they manifested greater piety toward the Egyptian gods than the Egyptians themselves. Around the middle of the seventh century B.C. Egypt managed to regain independence and rebuild a unified state under its own kings, a revival it enjoyed until 525. That year Persia swept in to add the land to its vast empire, and Persia held it, with some intervals, until 332, when Egypt fell to Alexander the Great during his relentless take-over of Persia's domains.

On Alexander's death in 323 his empire was torn apart as his generals warred against each other for pieces of it. Egypt was seized by Ptolemy, one of the most able of the generals, and by 300 B.C. he had established a dynasty that was to last for well-nigh three hundred years. Unlike the Nubian pharaohs, who revered Egypt and its ways, or the Persians, who were tolerant overlords and did little meddling, the Ptolemies quickly made their presence felt: they reduced the Egyptians, a people who once thought of themselves as superior to all others, to an underclass.

Prudently, the Ptolemies left Egypt's ancient way of life undisturbed. They presented themselves to the populace in the traditional trappings of the pharaoh and displayed due respect for the native gods by contributing to the maintenance of the temples and by building new ones. Just as they had for millennia, Egypt's priests carried on the daily religious routines and celebrated the great festivals, and Egypt's peasants cultivated their fields and rendered thanks to the gods for a favorable Nile flood. But the Egyptian population as a whole, from lordly cleric to humble worker, was reduced to second-class status: over it was imposed a layer of Greek society.

The Ptolemies wanted fellow Greeks to staff the important posts in their government and fill the ranks of their army and navy. They imported them from all over the Greek-speaking world—administrators for their new central bureaucracy, engineers to carry out their agricultural improvements, architects to design their new buildings, soldiers and sailors for their armed forces. From the Greek-speaking world also came a flood of others, from sober businessmen to wild-eyed adventurers, all eager to take advantage of the opportunities they perceived in an Egypt under Greek rule. These newcomers became part of an officially recognized privileged class, whose language was now not only the language of Egypt's government but of its business and commerce.

Before long there were communities of Greeks throughout much of Lower Egypt. Alexandria, the city founded by Alexander, chosen by the first Ptolemy as his capital, and built up by him and his immediate successors into a mighty commercial and cultural metropolis, was totally Greek: its life-style and appearance were Greek, it ruled itself by institutions that were Greek, it limited the citizen body to Greeks alone. In the district capitals lived the Greeks who served as function-aries in the Ptolemies' administration plus those who settled down there, since the capitals were good places to do business. Some Greeks even made their homes in rural villages. Wherever they were, whether in the purely Greek atmosphere of Alexandria or surrounded by Egyp-tian neighbors, they carried on a Greek life, speaking Greek, dwelling in Greek-style houses, following Greek social practices.

From about the end of the third century B.C. on, cracks appeared in the barrier between Greek and Egyptian as Greek men, particularly in rural areas, now and then took Egyptian wives. In 217 a military crisis forced the Ptolemies to recruit a sizable unit of Egyptian soldiers, and from then on Egyptians were accepted in the army, though they never enjoyed all the privileges of the non-Egyptian troops. But by and large, as long as the Ptolemaic dynasty held the throne, the Greeks remained a favored upper class, the Egyptians an oppressed underclass.

That dynasty was brought to an end by the Romans when, in 31 B.C., the forces of Augustus defeated those of Mark Antony and Cleopatra and, a year later, the queen pressed an asp to her bosom to avoid the humiliation of being paraded as a captive by her conquerors. She was the last of the Ptolemies, for, at her death, Egypt ceased to be a kingdom; Augustus reduced it to a province of the Roman empire under the governorship of an official appointed by the emperor.

The shift from Greek to Roman rule did nothing to help the Egyp-tians and much to worsen the lot of the Greeks. A new, uppermost, stratum of society came into existence made up of resident Roman citizens, the largest block of whom were the soldiers of two legions permanently stationed in Egypt. The next stratum consisted of the Greeks who were citizens of Alexandria or of a few other cities that, like it, had been Greek from the outset. The rest of the Greeks—even those who could trace their ancestry back to the early days of the Ptolemies—were more or less lumped together with the native population. They did not let this affect their way of life; they stubbornly clung to the social and cultural distinctions that marked them as Greek. Their com-munities kept up their theaters and their Greek-style temples, kept up the traditional youth organizations and athletic contests, kept up the *gymnasia,* the centers of Greek education and culture. At the same time intermarriage between Greeks and Egyptians became increasingly common, and it was not unusual for the children of these unions to have two names, one Greek and one Egyptian. Some did try to slough off the marks of their Egyptianness; thus, in a papyrus document that has survived, a man with the Greek name Eudaimon, who had been officially inscribed in the records as "son of Psois and Tiathres," formally petitioned to have that changed to "son of Heron and Didyme," switching the nomenclature of his parents from their Egyptian to their Greek names. "I will be benefitted," he asserts, although it is hard to see in what respect, outside of his *amour propre.*

The Ptolemies, everlastingly in need of funds to pay for their ambitious building plans, their lavish support of Greek culture, and above all the incessant warfare they carried on with the neighboring empire of the Seleucids, had squeezed the money out of their subjects by taxation which was particularly hard on the Egyptian population. The Romans went further: to them the land was purely and simply a source of revenue, and they taxed it mercilessly and with Roman efficiency.

Before Roman rule became destructively oppressive, Egypt, like the rest of the Roman empire, reaped the benefits of the celebrated Pax Romana, or Roman Peace, which lasted roughly two hundred years, from the inception of the empire in 27 B.C. to the close of the second century A.D. During this period Rome's well-organized administration and powerful armed forces gave the Mediterranean world not only political unity but also the longest span of unbroken peace in its history. As a consequence, travel became easier and safer than it had ever been, and this in turn caused trade to thrive on land and sea. Along with those who traveled for commercial or business reasons were some who traveled for its own sake—tourists. And Egypt, the land boasting the world's mightiest works of man, was one of the favored destinations.

Sightseeing in Egypt goes back, as we have noted in Chapter XII, to the days of the New Kingdom, as evidenced by the graffiti that Egyptian scribes and priests of that age left on the walls of the tombs and chapels they had visited. The first indication of foreign sightseers dates to 591 B.C. In that year a contingent of Greek mercenaries, hired by the pharaoh to help suppress an insurrection in Sudan, on their way passed the temple of Ramses II at Abu Simbel with its four gigantic seated figures of Ramses adorning the façade, and a number of the men scratched their names on his legs. Around 450 B.C., Herodotus, that indefatigable traveler, made an extensive trip to Egypt, one that provided the material for the long section on the country in his *Histories.* His words reveal that Egypt's reputation as the land of religion par excellence and its exotic ways was more of a lure for him than its monuments. He saw the monuments—it was impossible not to—but they made no great claim on his attention. When shown into one of the courts of the huge temple complex at Karnak, he remarked simply, "It's big." In describing the Great Pyramid, he dwelt at length not on its size but on the way it was built and how much it had cost.

During the tranquil and prosperous years of the Pax Romana sightseeing grew from a random activity into a regular tourist trade as visitors in numbers came to see the pyramids, the massive temples, the colossal statues, and Egypt's other memorabilia. The tourists arrived, with few exceptions, by ship at Alexandria, and they got a foretaste of what was in store for them even before they landed. While still out at sea, they could catch a glimpse of one of the Seven Wonders of the Ancient World, the lofty lighthouse of Alexandria visible thirty miles away. The city itself was well worth a look, with its splendid palaces and wide boulevards, but most people had not come for the likes of these. What they had come for lay miles further south.

Egypt's tourist attractions were along or near the Nile, a factor that made matters convenient, since the long distances between them could be covered by boat. The first important stop was Memphis, where travelers left the river to trudge or ride some fifteen miles to take in another of the Seven Wonders—the great pyramids. These were even more impressive then than now, for they were still entirely sheathed in their smooth veneer, of which only a scant bit about the apex of the pyramid of Khafre survives today.

Next in renown to the pyramids were the monuments in the vicinity of Thebes some four hundred miles south of Memphis. Here was Egypt's extra-special tourist attraction, the statue of Memnon. This is a colossal seated figure that we now know represents Amenhotep III but which the ancients believed was of Memnon, a mythological hero, son of the Goddess of Dawn, who appears briefly in the story of the Trojan War. He was king of the Ethiopians, and at some point late in the war he came with an army to help the Trojans and was slain by Achilles, leaving his mother grief-stricken. Plenty of colossal statues stood in Egypt, but none like Memnon's—it talked. Sometime around 27 B.C., an earthquake had caused its upper part to break off and fall to the ground, and thereafter at dawn—only at dawn—it made a sharp cracking sound, like the snapping of the string of a musical instrument. The conviction arose that this was Memnon having a conversation with his mother, and a dawn trip to overhear it became a must for tourists. The proof is on the statue's legs—from the base to as high as a person can reach, they are covered with graffiti recording visitors' astonishment at the remarkable experience. Some of the visitors were simple and direct: "I heard the wonderful Memnon along with my wife . . . and my children . . . 11 Choiak, 15th year of Hadrian [7 December A.D. 130]." Others went on at great length and effusively, including a good many who, finding prose insufficiently elevated to express their feelings, turned to verse. Sixty-one of the graffiti are in Greek and forty-five in Latin; they were left by people of all ranks, from ordinary travelers to the wife of the emperor Hadrian, and they range in date from the reign of Tiberius (A.D. 14–38) to A.D. 205. None are later; about A.D. 205 the emperor Septimius Severus ordered the part that had fallen off to be replaced, and this seems to have struck the statue dumb. The graffiti, unlike the usual run of such writings, are carefully carved inscriptions. Apparently, space on Memnon was allotted only to those who were willing to hire skilled stonecutters to put their messages on him.

After hearing Memnon perform at dawn, sightseers moved to the Valley of the Kings, a short walk away. Here the pharaohs of the New Kingdom had been laid to rest in tombs tunneled deep into the rock.

Though each tomb had been scrupulously sealed and its entrance left blank, long before Roman times robbers had found and broken into most, stripped them bare, and left them open; by the end of the first century B.C. at least forty were known. Of these, ten were visited by tourists. The proof, as in Memnon's case, is the graffiti they left on the walls. There are over two thousand, of which the great majority date from the time of the Pax Romana, plus a few that are earlier and a trickle that goes on until the Arab conquest of Egypt. Unlike those of Memnon, they are typical short tourist graffiti, most of them scratched with a sharp point and the rest done with reed pen and ink. They record, in addition to the visitors' names and often their homes, their reactions—the standard expression is "I saw and I was amazed." The majority are clustered near the entrances to the tombs, where there was natural light available, but some are deep in the bowels and must have been done under the light of torches. The tomb with the greatest number, almost half of all that have been found, is that of Ramses VI; people flocked to it because it was thought to be Memnon's. The tomb of Ramses IV is the runner-up with about a third of the total, no doubt because it was conveniently located near the entrance to the valley.

Visitors to Egypt could count on an ample range of tourist services. There were guides wherever needed. They led the sightseers from the shore at Memphis to the pyramids, from the shore at Thebes to Memnon, from Memnon to the Valley of the Kings, from tomb to tomb in the valley, down into and out of each tomb, and so on. They explained to them, in Greek or Latin as required, what they were seeing, embellishing their talks with fanciful details, as is the way with guides whether ancient or modern. There very likely were vendors hanging around the groups offering water or snacks and perhaps filling other needs, such as supplying pointed instruments or reed pens and ink to those inspired to inscribe a graffito. At certain places tourists could look forward to special performances put on for their delectation. A good show was available at the sanctuaries of the sacred crocodiles, where the priests had taught their charges to come up on call, open their mouths, and get their teeth cleaned and dried. At the sanctuary of the crocodile that incarnated Suchus, the crocodile god, a visitor could bring a special dish of pastry and meat and a bottle of wine and look on while the priest fed the food to the beast and flushed it down with the wine. At Memphis, where the sacred Apis bull was kept, visitors were allowed to watch the animal being exercised in an inner courtyard. A spectacular tourist show took place at the pyramids: agile men from a nearby village would shin up the smooth surface of the veneered face right to the very tip.

Egypt's flourishing days as a tourist center were a product of the Pax Romana, and they ended when that age was brought to a close by the troubles that descended upon the Roman empire soon after the opening of the third century A.D., the barbarian invasions from outside the borders and the political turmoil within. There followed nearly a century of unrest during which travel was at a low ebb. Around the beginning of the fourth century, Diocletian and Constantine, powerful and able emperors, restored stability to the Roman world. By this time that world was undergoing radical change as it became ever more Christianized.

In Egypt the coming of Christianity had a profound effect. All through the centuries of Greek and Roman rule, the native Egyptians, particularly the peasantry, had clung to their ancient ways, continuing to speak Egyptian and to worship the traditional gods. But the new religion called to them: by the middle of the fourth century it was the dominant faith, and its places of worship began to rise on grounds once sacred to the likes of Amon and Hathor. Egypt adopted a form of Christianity all its own, one that used Egyptian as the language of the church and not Greek, as elsewhere in the east. At the same time it gave rise to an institution that spread far beyond its borders—monasticism. The prime mover was St. Anthony: born around A.D. 250 in middle Egypt, at age nineteen he gave away his property and, after having lived an ascetic existence for fifteen years, retired from the world to dwell in isolation and spend his time in meditation, prayer, and struggle against the desires of the flesh. His example drew others, who settled as clusters of hermits around him and under his leadership. They were the world's first monks. When in the fifth century tourists again started coming to

Egypt, they were chiefly pilgrims who, having done the sights of the Holy Land, added an excursion to Egypt to visit its hermits, by this time numbering in the thousands and celebrated for their holiness.

In A.D. 640 the Arab invasion swept into Egypt. The ancient land was to have yet another set of foreign rulers, and, with them, a new religion.

Epilogue

The Egyptians were political pioneers. So far as we know, they were the first to create a unified state, to design governmental machinery for administering hundreds of miles and thousands of people, to plan and execute large projects.

They were also social pioneers. It was they who first worked out ways of gracious living, of enjoying leisure, of giving life an overlay of sophistication. It is in Egypt that we find the first houses that offer space and comfort, are handsomely decorated, and boast such amenities as baths and toilets. It is in Egypt that we first find serious attention given to the preparation of food, where the arts of cooking, baking, and brewing came to be developed and appreciated. It is Egypt that provides the earliest examples of dinner parties with their traditional features—elegant dress, efficient and courteous service, choice and abundant food, entertainment to amuse the guests. The ubiquitous tombs with their grave furniture and mummies give a wrong impression. The Egyptians were a worldly, materialistic people who, along with the somber monuments to their dead and their gods, bequeathed to posterity the art of adding refinement to daily living.

One art they did not enjoy, despite the bloodthirsty pronouncements of their pharaohs, was the art of war. Their rulers achieved many military victories (though not nearly as many as they claimed), but very often they did so by leading foreign troops or Egyptians stiffened by foreign contingents. Unfortunately, Egypt had neighbors who did enjoy war, and when for various reasons her powers grew steadily more feeble, these finally took away her independence. Nubians, Assyrians, Persians, Greeks, Romans—all made her in turn their vassal. From the middle of the fourth century B.C. on, Egypt's history ceases to be her own and becomes part of the history of the nations to which she belonged.

Chronological Table

Based on D. Silverman, ed., *Ancient Egypt* (New York 1997) 20–39.

Predynastic Period	Before 3000 B.C.
Early Dynastic Period	3000–2625
Old Kingdom (Third–Eighth Dynasties)	2625–2130
First Intermediate Period	
(Ninth–Tenth Dynasties)	2130–1980
Middle Kingdom	
(Eleventh–Thirteenth Dynasties)	1980–1630
Second Intermediate Period	1630–1539
New Kingdom	
(Eighteenth–Twentieth Dynasties)	1539–1075
Eighteenth Dynasty:	
Ahmose	1539–1514
Amenhotep I	1514–1493
Thutmose I	1493–1482

Thutmose II	1482–1479
Thutmose III	1479–1425
Hatshepsut	1479–?1458
Amenhotep II	1425–1400
Thutmose IV	1400–1390
Amenhotep III	1390–1353
Amenhotep IV (Akhenaten)	1353–1336
Nefernefruaten, Smenkhkare	1336–1332
Tutankhamen	1332–1322
Ay	1322–1319
Horemheb	1319–1292
Nineteenth Dynasty	
Ramses I	1292–1290
Seti I	1290–1279
Ramses II	1279–1213
Twentieth Dynasty	
Ramses III– XI	1187–1075

Abbreviations

Aldred (1968)	C. Aldred, *Akhenaten, Pharaoh of Egypt* (New York 1968).
Aldred (1988)	C. Aldred, *Akhenaten, King of Egypt* (London 1988).
ANET	J. Pritchard, ed., *Ancient Near Eastern Texts Relating to the Old Testament*[2] (Princeton 1955).
ARE	J. Breasted, ed., *Ancient Records of Egypt* (Chicago 1906).
CAH	*Cambridge Ancient History.*
Casson	L. Casson, *Travel in the Ancient World*[2] (Baltimore 1994).
Černý	J. Černý, *Ancient Egyptian Religion* (London 1952).
Drioton-Vandier	E. Drioton and J. Vandier, *L'Égypte*[6] (Paris 1984).
Emery	W. Emery, *Archaic Egypt* (Baltimore 1961).
Erman	A. Erman, *The Literature of the Ancient Egyptians* (London 1927).
Gardiner	A. Gardiner, *Egypt of the Pharaohs* (Oxford 1961).
Glanville	S. Glanville, *Daily Life in Ancient Egypt* (London 1930).

Harris   J. Harris, *The Legacy of Egypt*[2] (Oxford 1971).

Hayes   W. Hayes, *The Scepter of Egypt* (New York 1953, 1959).

Kees   E. Kees, *Ancient Egypt: A Cultural Topography* (Chicago 1961).

Lucas-Harris   A. Lucas and J. Harris, *Ancient Egyptian Materials and Industries*[4] (London 1962).

Montet   P. Montet, *La vie quotidienne en Égypte au temps des Ramsès* (Paris 1946).

Nunn   J. Nunn, *Ancient Egyptian Medicine* (London 1996).

Posener   G. Posener, *Dictionary of Egyptian Civilization* (London 1962).

Pritchard   J. Pritchard, *The Near East in Pictures* (Princeton 1954).

Riefstahl   E. Riefstahl, *Thebes in the Time of Amunhotep III* (Norman, Okla. 1964).

Sigerist   H. Sigerist, *A History of Medicine,* i (Oxford 1951).

Silverman   D. Silverman, *Ancient Egypt* (New York 1997).

Wilson   J. Wilson, *The Culture of Ancient Egypt* (Chicago 1951).

Notes

Chapter I. The New Kingdom

4–6 Menes: Wilson 43. Nature of the Old Kingdom: Wilson 67. "This land is helter-skelter": *ANET* 445. "Why, really, the land spins": *ANET* 441. Robbing royal tombs: Wilson 109. "To whom can I speak": *ANET* 406. Rise of Thebes: Wilson 125–126. Middle Kingdom pharaoh's image: Wilson 132. Hyksos: Wilson 155, 161, 163.

Chapter II. The Social Pyramid

10–11 Egypt's pyramidal society: Wilson 73. Small landholders: Wilson 128. Pharaoh's religious duties: Montet 189–194. Royal toilet: Montet 194–196. Tossing of gold necklaces: Montet 201. Reception of embassies: Montet 204–205.

11–13 Vizier as early as Fourth Dynasty: Drioton-Vandier 147. Vizier's duties: Hayes in *CAH*³ ii, Part 1.354–357. Mayors as provincial officials: *CAH*³ ii, Part 1.357. Viceroy of Nubia: *CAH*³ ii, Part 1.348–349. Temple-owned land: Wilson 271. Court officials: Hayes in *CAH*³ ii, Part 1.360–362. Hatshepsut's favorite courtier: Wilson 171–172. Inheriting of offices: Wilson 171.

14–16 Amenhotep III's palace accommodations: Riefstahl 65–67. Workers' housing at Thebes: Riefstahl 69–73. Ancient Egypt's population: Riefstahl 180–181.

Chapter III. The Family

17–18 "If thou art a man": *ANET* 413. Brother-sister marriage: Wilson 97. Wife furnishes one-third, husband two-thirds: Montet 54. "Take to thyself a wife": *ANET* 420. Importance of children: Montet 60–61. Toys: Glanville 18. Greek vs. Egyptian attitudes: Montet 61. Name, horoscope, registry, mother's care: Montet 61–64. "Her breast was in thy mouth": *ANET* 420–421.

19–21   Tell el Amarna homes: T. Peet and C. Woolley, *Egyptian Exploration Society Memoirs* 38 (1923) 37–50. Gardens, middle-class housing: Montet 28–30. Workers' village: Hayes i, 257. Workers' housing at Tell el Amarna: Peet-Woolley 55–67.

21–22   Recipes against pests: Montet 31. Furniture, dinnerware: Montet 32–34. Folding stools, low stools: Hayes ii, 202. Beds, cupboards: Hayes ii, 203. Workers' houses: Hayes ii, 405. Servants, slaves: Wilson 187; Montet 65–68. Use of the stick: Montet 68. Pets: Montet 69–72. Brindled tabby: Hayes i, 224.

22–25   Telling time: Montet 43–46. "They always wear": Herodotus 2.37. Use of soda, ointments against drying: Sigerist 246. Pine oil, incense: Montet 74. Pomade cones: Montet 77, 97. Barbering, hairdressing, make-up: Montet 73–74; Sigerist 246. Beauty aids: Montet 74–75. Castor oil plant: Sigerist 340–341. "to cause hair to grow": Nunn 149. Recipes for gray hair, "were probably as effective": Sigerist 247. Fenugreek, "change an old man," shaven heads: Montet 75. Dress: Montet 76–78. Sinuhe: *ANET* 22. Jewelry: Hayes ii, 179–187.

25–26   Cooking, baking: Montet 86–90. Beer, wine: Montet 90–91. Beef, poultry, fish, vegetables: Montet 79–86. Illumination: Montet 93–94; Kees 77; Hayes i, 260–261. "everyone owns a net": Herodotus 2.95.

Chapter IV. Women

27–30   Daughter, wife, mother of a god: Wilson 96–97. Pepi II, Nitocris: Gardiner 101–102. "she had a large underground chamber": Herodotus 2.100. "the noblest and loveliest": Manetho, *Aegyptiaca* Fr. 21(a). Hatshepsut: Wilson 174–177; Gardiner 183–188. Tiy: Wilson 201–203. Received communications: *CAH*³ ii, Part 1.483.

30–34   Harem intrigues: Wilson 157–158; Montet 212–214. Harem of Mentuhotep II: Hayes i, 160–161. Concubines: Riefstahl 114. "have the housemaid": Wilson 130. Wives and husbands seated separately: Montet 97. "May I be sent": Glanville 16. Beating of wives: Montet 59. "rose to the highest rank": Montet 58. Adultery: Montet 59; Posener, s.v. "marriage." Women in Egyptian literature: Montet 55–57. "Be on thy guard": *ANET* 420. "Thou shouldst not supervise": *ANET* 421. Husband and wife share activities: Montet 101 (parties), 102 (games), 60 (hunting). Legal rights: Wilson 203; cf. *ANET* 216. "Seven days to yesterday": *ANET* 468–469. "Though he lives close by": Montet 51–52.

Chapter V. On the Farm

35–37   "Egypt . . . is . . . the gift": Herodotus 2.5. "When the Nile inundates": Herodotus 2.97. "black land," "red land": Gardiner 27. Three seasons: Kees 48, 54–55. Nilometers: Kees 50–52, 310. Types of land: Kees 53–54. "held up the water," "built a dam": *ANET* 34.

37–38   Wheat and barley: Kees 74. Sow and then plow: Montet 111. Trample in the seed: Montet 114. Harvesting: Montet 115–118. "Give me just a handful": Montet 118. Girls fighting: Wilson 147–148. Threshing, punishment for cheating: Montet 120.

38–39   Flax, castor oil, beans, etc.: Kees 77–78. Papyrus: N. Lewis, *Papyrus in Classical Antiquity* (Oxford 1974) 21–31 (uses), 34–69 (making of paper), 84–94 (export). "Make for me": *ANET* 407. Farm activities: Hayes i, 264.

39–41   Amon's animal holdings: Wilson 270. Branding: Montet 126. Beefy cattle and scrawny herdsman: Wilson fig. 15a. Model of stalls, slaughterhouse: Hayes i, 263–264. Goats, sheep, pigs, etc.: Kees 90–91. "The tenant-farmer": *ANET* 433. "A good day," "This good day," "Thresh ye for yourselves": *ANET* 469.

Chapter VI. At Leisure

42–46   First Dynasty board games: Hayes i, 45. *senet:* Hayes i, 250; ii, 198–200. Hounds and jackals: Hayes i, 250. Husband vs. wife, watched by children: Montet 102. Greeting guests: Montet 95–96. Seating: Montet 96–97. "Drink till thou art drunk," "Give me eighteen measures," "Drink!": Montet 101. Vomiting: Montet 101–102. "one of those sitting": *ANET* 412. "any place where thou mightest enter": *ANET* 413. Musical instruments: Montet 98–99; Pritchard figs. 206–209. Dancing: Posener, s.v. "dancing;" Pritchard figs. 209–211. Songs: Montet 99–100. "Follow thy desire": *ANET* 467.

46–49   Marsh hunts: Montet 130. Desert hunts: Montet 131–133. Big game: Montet 208–209. "Never was the like," "said this without boasting": *ANET* 240. "He hunted 120 elephants": *ANET* 241. "seven lions by shooting": *ANET* 243. Amenhotep II's shooting: Wilson 198. His hunting: Montet 133. His training of horses: Wilson 196–197. Ramses III's hunting: Montet 209. Run 20 miles before breakfast: Diodorus 1.53.3. "after they had attained": *ANET* 244. Horseplay on the water: Montet 128. Water jousting: P. Montet, *Les scènes de la vie privée dans les tombeaux égyptiens de l'Ancien Empire* (Paris 1925) 82. Tug-of-war: Wilson fig. 10a. Leapfrog: Montet 103. Leather balls, tipcat: Hayes i, 251. Girls' games: Montet 104.

Chapter VII. The Professions

50–51 "Be a scribe": *ANET* 432. Pens behind their ears: Pritchard fig. 232. Scribes in fields: Montet 120. In slaughterhouses: Hayes i, 263. In army compounds: Montet 226. At trials: Pritchard fig. 231. Tallying severed hands: Pritchard fig. 340. Scribe in squad of sailors: Hayes i, 69. Temple estates: Wilson 270–271.

51–53 "cannot breathe," "fingers are foul," "sides ache," "is dirtier," "after he has made over," "the Delta to get trade": *ANET* 433. Six hundred signs: Riefstahl 85. Scribe enrolled at five: Montet 247. Schooling: Riefstahl 86–87; Montet 248–249. "The teaching that maketh clever": Ermann 187. Copying of classics: Wilson 262. Urging own whipping: Erman 188.

53–55 Writing materials: Montet 248. "a youngster's ear": Montet 249. "I hear that you are neglecting": Erman 190–191. Uni, Nekhebu, "When I accompanied": Wilson 89–90. Amenhotep-son-of-Hapu: Gardiner 209–210. Graft: Wilson 279. Crooked riverboat captain: Wilson 280.

56–60 "He carries his bread": Montet 217. Old Kingdom and Middle Kingdom army: Hayes i, 277. Foreign troops: Kees 141–142. Egyptian weapons: Hayes i, 277–284. Hyksos weaponry: Wilson 163. New Kingdom army: Drioton-Vandier 455–456. Supply: Montet 220. *Medjai:* Wilson 137–138. Asiatics, Libyans in Egypt's army: Kees 142–143. Military class: Drioton-Vandier 457. No integration: Montet 223–224. Advancement: Wilson 187–188; Montet 218–220.

60–61 "are skilled beyond all men": *Od.* 4.231–232. Egyptian doctors in foreign service: Nunn 131–132. Administrative titles: Nunn 116–117. "overseer of the female doctors": Nunn 124. "doctors of the palace," "chief of the doctors of the palace," etc.: Nunn 117–118. Herodotus on specialization: 2.84. Specialization characteristic of primitive medicine: Sigerist 319. Egyptian specialists: Nunn 119. Irenakhty: Nunn 126–127. Dentists: Nunn 119. Veterinarians: Nunn 119–120; Sigerist 300–301. Apprenticeship: Nunn 130–131. Edwin Smith papyrus and Ebers papyrus could be texts: Nunn 131. "students from among": Sigerist 324.

62–64 Palace physicians: Nunn 117–118. Physicians at state institutions: Sigerist 321. Magical-religious medicine: Sigerist 272. Magicians as doctors: Nunn 98. "O, ghost": Sigerist 275. Exact execution: Sigerist 274–275. Amulets: Sigerist 282–283. Development of true pharmacology: Sigerist 284. Egypt's materia medica: Nunn 136–162. Demond-discouraging mixtures: Sigerist 275, 342. Honey: Nunn 148.

64–67 Edwin Smith papyrus: Nunn 25–30. "Instructions for a gaping wound": Nunn 27. "an ailment which I will treat," etc.: Nunn 28. For use by army surgeons: Sigerist 310. Ebers papyrus: Nunn 30–34. "too oppressed to eat," etc.: Sigerist 327. Observation: Sigerist 327. "weak like a breath," etc.: Sigerist 327. "what is lifted by cough," "like pig's blood": Sigerist 328. "a very large swelling": Sigerist 328–329. "goes and comes," "His heart beats": Sigerist 329. Meat on wounds, poultices: Sigerist 344. "two . . . bandages of linen": Nunn 173. Splints: Nunn 176–177. Healed fractures: Nunn 177. Prosthetic dentistry: Sigerist 346–347. Preparation of prescriptions: Nunn 139–143. Honey-candy, bread pills: Sigerist 337. "For a dislocation": Sigerist 338. Galen, Dioscorides: Sigerist 357. Wheat and barley: Nunn 191–192.

68–71 "Cheops . . . put all the Egyptians": Herodotus 2.124–125. 755 feet: Silverman 174. Handling of blocks: Harris 103–104. Egyptian arithmetic: Wilson 71–72. Imhotep: Gardiner 72–73. Senmut: Wilson 172.

Chapter VIII. Fine Craftsmen

72–74 Stone vessels: Lucas-Harris 421–428. Woodworking: Emery 216–222; Lucas-Harris 449–454. Inlay, veneer: Lucas-Harris 454. Six-layer plywood: Lucas-Harris 451. Glues: Lucas-Harris 3. Bent wood: Lucas-Harris 451.

74–76 Linen: Emery 222–224. Leather: Lucas-Harris 33–37. Copper: Lucas-Harris 199–217; J. Muhly, *Copper and Tin* (Hamden, Conn. 1973) 217–220. "This land was reached": *ANET* 229. Wire: Emery 226. Statue of Pepi I: Lucas-Harris 214–215. Caravan trade in tin: Muhly 292–293. No tin in Iran: Muhly, Supplement 97–98. Afghanistan deposits: S. Cleuziou and T. Berthoud, "Early Tin in the Near East," *Expedition* 25.1 (Fall 1982) 14–19. Iron: Lucas-Harris 235–243. Gold: Lucas-Harris 224–232. First Dynasty tomb: Emery 228. Ten thousand ounces, 150 porters: *CAH*[3] ii, Part 1.350.

77–78 Stone quarrying and working: Lucas-Harris 63–74. Relief of colossus: R. Engelbach in S. Glanville, *The Legacy of Egypt* (Oxford 1942) 146. Inlaid eyes: Lucas-Harris 99–100, 107–109. Paint pigments, vehicle: Lucas-Harris 338–353. Varnish: Lucas-Harris 356–361.

79–82 Akhenaten's chief sculptor and assistants: Kees 300–302. Housing at Thebes: Riefstahl 72–73. "each one of you": Kees 169. Hierarchy of workers: Riefstahl 70. Kha: Riefstahl 72. Tomb at Thebes: Montet 157–

158. Gifts of property, etc.: *CAH*[3] ii, Part 1.379. Sick leave: Sigerist 259. Leave for nursing the sick: F. Jonckheere, *Chronique d'Égypte* 20, nos. 39–40 (Jan.–July 1945), 32. Beaten by his wife: Jonckheere 31. Strike at Thebes: Wilson 275–277; cf. Sigerist 246. "The worst of fates": Agatharchides 24–26.

Chapter IX. Religion

83–86   "The Egyptians consider": Herodotus 2.65–69. Early animal worship: Černý 19–20. Palaces of mud brick: Harris 101. Officials are prelates: Wilson 171. Senmut's religious titles: Wilson 172. Anthropomorphism: Černý 27–28. Ptah portrayed as human: Černý 30. Creation myth: Wilson 59–60.

86–91   Re, Heliopolis: Wilson 87–88; Riefstahl 128–130; Kees 155–156. Amon: Wilson 130–141; Riefstahl 135–137. Karnak: Kees 257–260. Amon's wealth: Wilson 270–271. Pharaoh's nature: Wilson 47–50. Osiris, Isis, Horus: Riefstahl 130–133. Spread of Isis worship: Harris 153–155. Sekhmet: Kees 160; Nunn 101. Bes, Thoueris: Riefstahl 75. Foreign gods: Wilson 191–192. "the cosmic form of harmony": Wilson 48–49. Egyptian character: Wilson 145–153.

91–93   Limestone vs. sandstone: Harris 103. The temple community: Montet 270–271, 290–291. Succession of buildings at Karnak: *CAH*[3] ii, Part 1.391–393; Kees 272. Luxor: *CAH*[3] ii, Part 1.395–396. Ramses' 56-foot statue: Kees 273. Ramses' cannibalizing: Kees 198.

93–96   Temple routine: Montet 273–274; Riefstahl 151. Clergy: Riefstahl 153–157. Training, appointment of priests: Riefstahl 152–153. Ptahmose, Amenhotep-son-of-Hapu: Riefstahl 157. Votives, healing steles: Montet 274. Workmen's shrines: Montet 275–276.

96–99   New Year's festival: Riefstahl 159. "The Egyptians celebrate": Herodotus 2.59–60. Feast of Opet: Riefstahl 162–166; Montet 283–286. Feast of the Valley: Montet 286–287. Putting questions to the god: Montet 277. Young Thutmose: *CAH*[3] ii, Part 1.328. Necropolis workers' festival: Montet 276. *Sed* festivals: Riefstahl 160–161. Amenhotep III's *Sed* festivals: *CAH*[3] ii, Part 1.345.

Chapter X. A Maverick Pharaoh

100–101   Amenhotep III as hunter: Riefstahl 78–79. "lord of strength," "fierce-eyed lion": *CAH*[3] ii, Part 1.340. Asiatic brides: *CAH*[3] ii, Part 1.345–346. Amenhotep III as builder: *CAH*[3] ii, Part 1.340–342.

101–103 Akhenaten's earliest portraits traditional: Aldred (1968) 210. Sun disk long established in Egyptian religion: Wilson 210–211. *"Splendor of Aten"*: *CAH*³ ii, Part 1.343. Aten temple at Karnak: Aldred (1988) 264. Iconoclastic portrayals have features of sun worship: Aldred (1988) caption to plates 33–35. "the vivid imagination": Aldred (1968) 14. New capital: *CAH*³ ii, Part 2.55–59. Single deity approached through Akhenaten: Wilson 223. Striking out of gods' names: Wilson 221.

103–112 Amarna art: *CAH*³ ii, Part 2.93–96; Wilson 193–194, 217–220. "Thou appearest beautifully": *ANET* 370. Breasted's view of Akhenaten: *The Dawn of Conscience* (New York 1933) 289–297 ("lonely idealist" 293–294, "god-intoxicated" 292). Akhenaten's hymn as source for Hebrew psalmist: Breasted 366–368. Akhenaten as social reformer: Aldred (1968) 257. Fröhlich's, Klinefelter's syndrome: Nunn 84. Amenhotep III father of Akhenaten's children: Aldred (1968) 137. Wilson's view of Akhenaten: 206–233. Akhenaten chose portrayal with curious characteristics: Aldred (1988) 234–235, 336. Nefertiti's name erased because of death: Aldred (1988) 230. Attacks on Amon late in realm, result of personal tragedies and public setbacks: Aldred (1988) 289–290. Horemheb's first year: Gardiner 241.

Chapter XI. The Afterlife

114–115 Fourth millennium B.C. burials: Wilson 26. Pharaoh's immortality shared by nobles, servants: Wilson 63–65. Democratization of immortality: Wilson 116–118. Short-lived moral aspect: Wilson 118–119.

115–118 How to ensure success in the underworld trial: Riefstahl 133. Section of Book of the Dead buried with corpse: Montet 296. "What is said on reaching": *ANET* 34. "O Breaker-of-Bones," etc.: *ANET* 35. "I have given bread," "This spell is to be recited": *ANET* 36. "O my heart": Montet 297.

118–120 Pharaoh accompanies the sun: Wilson 66. Living on in the underworld: Riefstahl 143–144. *ka, ba*: Riefstahl 144–145. *ushebtis,* "The Osiris So-and-So": Montet 303–304. Attitude toward death before and after 1200 B.C.: Wilson 296–297. A ritualistic, religion-haunted nation: Wilson 306–307. "There was constructed": *ANET* 22.

121–125 Rock-cut royal and nobles' tombs: *CAH*³ ii, Part 1.401–406. Tomb furniture, coffin, Canopic jars: Montet 302–303. "The embalmers": Herodotus 2.86–89. Results of examination of mummies: Lucas-Harris 299–326. Liberal use of resin: Lucas-Harris 296–297. Cheap burials, Egyptian potter's field: Montet 317. The funeral: Montet

311–316. Endowments for services for the dead: Montet 306–309. Effect of Old Kingdom endowments: Wilson 98–100. "They who build in granite": *ANET* 405.

Chapter XII. Travel

126–129   "I reached Elephantine": *ARE* i, nos. 611–612. Wadi Natrun: Lucas-Harris 263. Natron in mummification: Lucas-Harris 278–303. "to open up the way": Gardiner 99–100. Extent of Harkhuf's travels: Gardiner 101. Punt, Hatshepsut's expedition: Kees 110–115. "southern panther": *ARE* ii, no. 272. "Hard to port": *ARE* ii, no. 252. "Watch your step": *ARE* ii, no. 264.

129–135   Egyptian ships and boats: L. Casson, *Ships and Seamanship in the Ancient World*³ (Baltimore 1995) 11–22. Transport of Hatshepsut's obelisks: *CAH*³ ii, Part 1.331. Roads on dikes: Montet 168. Camels: Casson (*Travel*) 55–56. Chariots: Montet 169. Ferries: Montet 168. Denderites swim despite crocodiles: Strabo 17.1.44. Scribes as tourists: Casson (*Travel*) 32–33. Wenamon: *ANET* 25–29.

Chapter XIII. Egypt under Non-Egyptians

137–139   Ptolemies as pharaohs, status of Greeks: N. Lewis, *Greeks in Ptolemaic Egypt* (Oxford 1986) 4. Immigration to Egypt, its attractions: Lewis 15–21. Greek communities: Lewis 9–10. Intermarriage: Lewis 27–29. Citizenship under Roman rule: N. Lewis, *Life in Egypt under Roman Rule* (Oxford 1983) 19–35. Intermarriage more common, Eudaimon: Lewis (1983) 32.

140–142   Greek mercenaries at Abu Simbel: Casson 274–275. "It's big": Herodotus 2.143. Description of the Great Pyramid: Herodotus: 2.124–125. Alexandria: Casson 258. Memnon: Casson 272–278. Valley of the Kings: Casson 278–283.

142–144   Guides: e.g., the *hermeneus* "interpreter," who translated an inscription on the pyramid for Herodotus (2.125). Feeding of crocodiles, shinning up the pyramid: Casson 271. Apis bull: Casson 259. Christianity dominant by mid–fourth century A.D.: H. Bell, *Egypt, from Alexander the Great to the Arab Conquest* (Oxford 1948) 104. Christian tourists: Casson 310–314.

Index